The Entrepreneur's Curse

How to Avoid Disease and Early Death *Without* Sacrificing Your Happiness

Dr. HB Lo

The Entrepreneur's Curse: How to Avoid Disease and Early Death Without Sacrificing Your Happiness

Print ISBN: 9798375180977

Publisher: **Author Writer's Academy (AWA) Literary Agency, United States**

Senior Editor: Marjah Simon

www.AWA4Life.com

Cover Design, Illustrations, and Interior Layout by Author Writer's Academy

DISCLAIMER: The content in this book is intended for educational and entertainment purposes only. This book is not intended to be a substitute for the legal, medical, psychological, accounting, or financial advice of a professional. The author and publisher are not offering professional services advice. Additionally, this book is not intended to serve as the basis for any financial or business decisions. You should seek the services of a competent professional, especially if you need expert assistance for your specific situation.

Success stories and results shared are not typical and do not guarantee future results or performance. While best efforts

For your *Complimentary* Burnout Prevention Masterclass to accompany the incredible content in this book, while available, please visit https://www.drhblo.com/webinar

Table of Contents

DEDICATION IX

ACKNOWLEDGEMENT X

LETTER FROM THE AUTHOR XI

PART 1: THE SECRET EVERY ENTREPRENEUR NEED TO STAY SUCCESSFUL 15

CHAPTER 1 16

Listening To Your Subconscious 24

Action Items 1 30

CHAPTER 2 31

Our Ephemeral Needs 39

Finding the Answer Within You 43

Action Items 2 49

CHAPTER 3 50

Purifying the Body 54

The Hourglass Model 64

Purifying the Mind 76

Purifying the Spirit 89

Fortifying Your Breath 91

Fortifying Your Water 94

Fortifying your Food 97

Amplifying 101

Rituals - The Steady Platform 106

Rhythms - The Cycles on Top of the Platform 111

Amplifying Routines 113

Health Vision 115

Summary of Good Health 118

Action Items 3 122

PART 2: WORKING WITH YOUR SUBCONSCIOUS ... 125

CHAPTER 4 126

The Bliss Point 128

Marketing and Myths 131

How to Approach Health 135

How to 'Rewire' 140

Internal Over External Validation 144

Action Items 4 150

CHAPTER 5 152

Mind and Reality 155

What is Quantum Thinking? 156

Mind Loops, Explained 159

Getting Out of a Mind Loop 161

The Principles of Breaking Mind Loops 170

Health Visions and How to Realise Them 173

Conflict and Inversion 179

Action Items 5 186

CHAPTER 6 188

Peering into the Depths 195

Changing your Subconscious and Habits 202

The Gamma Brainwave State Exercise: 206

Action Items 6 208

CHAPTER 7 210

Why Are Things Hidden from Us? 213

Reconceptualising Feelings 217

Action Items 7 226

CHAPTER 8 228

Be Present 232

Let's Practise 236

You Can Be Stronger than Marketing 238

Be in Touch with your Baseline 243

Be in Touch with your Health Vision 244

Action Items 8 248

CHAPTER 9 250

Modifying Memories and Associations 255

Finding the Worms is the Biggest Step 260

Action Items 9 265

PART 3: YOUR OWN HEALTH PLAN 267

CHAPTER 10 268

Core Principles 269

CHAPTER 11 271

Week 1: Air 273

Week 2: Water 274

Week 3: Food 275

Week 4: Mind 276

Week 5: Spirit 277

Week 6: Body 278

CHAPTER 12 279

How to Track More Effectively 282

How to Know When You are Making Progress 283

Tracking Sheet 287

CONCLUSION 288

Fantasy 290

Reality 290

TESTIMONIALS 292

NEXT STEPS 300

ABOUT THE AUTHOR 301

Dedication

To my two shining lights, **Jason** and **Jessica**, my children

— you are the reasons I wake up each day and aim to do better.

Acknowledgement

To my wife **Tanya** without whose support life would lose all joy and meaning.

To my parents **Soo Khim** and **Guan Hwa** who continue to put up with my pie in the sky ideas and support me no matter how ridiculous my dreams. You literally gave life to my journey in health.

To my teacher **Chok** who taught me the secret to effortless high performance in any field was through cultivating love of the subject at hand.

Finally, to my **mentors past, present and emerging** who continually refine and help hone my imperfect knowledge of this miraculous living machine we call the human body.

Letter from the Author

Entrepreneurs, Executives, Presidents, Business people — you are amazing human beings, doing incredible things every day. You push the boundaries of your environment and decide for yourselves what is possible. You change lives. Without you, there would be no innovation, no progress, no special experiences that are born from service.

> I am so glad that you have decided to level up in the one thing that can either accelerate or completely derail all your accomplishments — your health.

Whether you are a 70-year-old arthritic business exec, a marathon running business owner at the very start of your career, or anything in-between, this book is going to show you unconventional ways to take your health up a notch.

So, what can you expect by taking this journey?

Well, it's hard to quantify, so perhaps the best way to display this is to showcase the results other people are getting. Be forewarned — results are individual. They are not a guarantee. Instead, they will depend on how your body responds when you start tapping into your own innate intuitive intelligence (don't worry, you'll learn about this as you explore further).

And what kind of results are possible when you do?

How about a 13-year-old reversing cancer? She received chemo that devastated her body, as well as radiation that further damaged her at a cellular level.

Now, reverse that.

She did, all in the space of six months, after three years of hell.

How about my 75-year-old spritely old lady, who had been on three opioid painkillers because of crippling arthritis, and walked with a cane?

She made just one change to her health habit, and within a month was walking aid-free. Within another month she was completely off the pain meds.

Incredible? Yes.

How about my twin asthmatic children who were on weekly steroids because their asthma was out of control. With just one habit change, they went from persistent asthma attacks to not even needing Ventolin.

How about my dear friend in university who had hay fever, which got so bad that his choice was to either have antihistamines strong enough to knock him out, or have his sinus stuffed so badly that he couldn't function. Not much of a choice there.

Again, through one simple habit change, he was allergy free. In fact, I vividly remember the day he broke the good news to me. He came strutting into the tutorial room and said, "Guess what I did today?" Then he announced that he had just strolled through freshly cut grass while it was being mowed, something he had not even been able to contemplate for the past decade.

How about, finally, my dear friend who took up my advice to have his cholesterol checked, even though he was at peak health, and was found to have 'dangerously high' cholesterol levels. His case was a little more complicated, but we were able to narrow down the causative factors.

Now his levels are normal, and he has never felt better, kicking butt as an executive and on track to become a CEO in the next five years. Though, admittedly, I can't claim any credit for that part; he is a genius who works exceptionally hard, as I am sure *you are* too.

The fact is, your body has tremendous capacity to heal. It is the only thing that ever has the ability to get you back to your healthy state; everything else is either an aid or a hindrance. Knowing this, my book will teach you how you can determine what helps and what doesn't, as you re- engage with your innate intuitive intelligence.

Now, you may have picked up this book because you are self-aware of your own sacrifice, having disregarded health in order to build wealth. Yet know that you are not alone. Not only have I been in your shoes, but also know many people who embarked upon their own journey as entrepreneurs to have felt exactly what you are currently.

Each one had the same focus and drive necessary in order to make the business successful, just as you do. However, what often led to the success of their business created exactly the wrong recipe for their long-term health success.

It is important to learn that bad health doesn't just affect you; it trickles down to the people around you. If you are a father or mother, your children are constantly learning lifelong habits that will either make or break their health.

As the CEO of a company, bad health affects not only the sharpness of your thinking, but in fact your ability to respond to challenges. The great news is that the challenge to improve your health can be easily solved. In fact, the answer is obvious you tap into the *inner* wellspring of information.

You have already likely looked everywhere for the answer, but still feel lost.

- Are you frustrated with all of the contradictory information, diets and food choices around you?
- Have you been disappointed with all the 'fast, magic pills' that simply do not work?
- Are you tired of doing 'all the right things' while still not getting the right results?
- Do you find yourself unable to maintain the demands of typical health plans?

- Are you getting progressively tired and rundown?
- Do you feel you are on the verge of burning out?
- Are you tired of various health plans and fad diets?
- Do you want a new, easy health track?

This book is for people who sense these worries. Who think, "Yeah, I've got to pay attention to myself." Whether you are sure you need to make a change, or have just begun to worry about your health, this book will act as your guide.

Yet how do you truly know if you're going down a path of bad health? Well, consider these additional questions:

- Do you have muscular pains that don't seem to go away?
- Are you experiencing extended, unexplainable stress?
- Are you yearning for a sense of peace?
- Are you wondering why you don't feel rested and rejuvenated, even after a good night's sleep?

These are bad signs, and perhaps more importantly, ones that can add up. Yet now is the time to realise that there *is* hope, and I am here to help you find it.

This is the LAST and ONLY health book you will ever need.

Yes, a big claim, but it is TRUE.

If I asked you:

What are 5 things you can do today that will immediately worsen your health?

What would you say? While I might not know your specific answers, I am certain that you would be able to respond with a range of them, whether dietary, exercise or lifestyle-related. No research would be required. No scientific studies. No doctor's advice. You would just *know*. At the same time, I am also certain that you probably engage with at least one of these habits every day.

The reverse is also true. Ask yourself:

What 5 things could I do today that will immediately lead to improved health in my life?

Similarly, you know the answers — so what is missing?

ACTION!

Consistent, Stackable, Sustainable action (CSS) is what is required to move from *knowing* into *doing*. And the most effective way to exact this change is to develop an automatic CSS habit.

In this book, you will learn how to listen for the clues your body is giving you; all you will then have to do is follow them. This treasure lies within all of us, and you simply need to know how to find it.

Unlike other fad diets and health books, I will not give you a strict plan. I will not give you exact steps to follow, nor will I tell you to immediately overhaul your entire life.

Instead, you will be able to incorporate good health habits into your life gradually, in a way that works for *you*. Every person who reads this book will come away with a personalised way to achieve optimal health, catered to one's own uniqueness, as indeed everyone should work on what is best for *them*.

Through this awareness and practice of honouring the steps I provide, you will experience a level of consistent health like never before. You will never wonder what to do again —you'll know.

Thank you for allowing me to be your guide, and here's to the start of reclaiming your inner intuition and optimal health.

Dr HB Lo

Introduction

This is not another 'how to' book telling you what to eat and what not to eat. Nor is it another book that will give you an entire set of 'rules' to follow. It will instead reveal to you the answers that you already know, setting you on your path to reclaim the intuitive capacities that you have lost touch with.

> *You will become healthy —*
> *not by me telling you how to live your life,*
> *but rather by allowing you to*
> *find the solutions within yourself.*

Instead of looking outwards to the sea of misinformation for answers, you will be guided back inwards. My end goal is to make every other health book or program obsolete. You should become your own lighthouse, showing yourself the way. And as you finish the material, you will be able to find out the answers, internally, to any health questions you have.

Thereafter, you can validate these answers based on your experience, your sensations, your imagination, and what is happening inside your body. You will no longer need external validation of any sort. Yet this can only happen if your mind is set straight, for only then will your body follow.

You are imperfectly perfect.

Sit on this for a week or so; contemplate the truth in this simple sentence. The inner perfection that is your inner intuitive intelligence actually knows what you need — it may just be dormant from inactivity. Innate intuitive intelligence is the knowledge you have inside you that you have lost touch with. It is the ability to understand what you really want, and what you really need to do, by accessing all the subconscious signals your body is giving you. And we are going to wake it up, so you can:

- Make optimal health decisions without being swayed by slick marketing messages
- Trust your smart, intelligent body signals
- Identify what you uniquely need to not just *survive,* but *thrive*
- Unleash your inner healer
- Create your personal map towards optimal health

This is a special book, not to be read like others, as the goal is to enable you to both think for and understand yourself, as opposed to merely teaching you the answers.

There are two parts to realising your goals. The first involves learning about the mind and how to use it for optimal health. This will allow you to get rid of the negative thoughts that hold you back, understand yourself on a whole new level, uncover your ability to find the right answers with your innate intuitive intelligence and be able to comprehend your subconscious (and perhaps even communicate back)!

The second involves observing the parallel physical results from the actual implementation of these mind principles. In doing so, you will be able to make correct decisions regarding your health, or anything for that matter. Then, as a result, you will be able to make changes to what you eat and how you live. Not because I tell you to, but because you will know what works for and is good for you, in turn making you *want* to do it! Thereafter, you will soon begin to notice the physical results of good health.

By learning, through this book, the things you can implement into your own life, you will begin to understand the ways in which your mind and body relate to one another. And by understanding your mind, your subconscious will show you the way to achieve the physical results you want, which will in turn have a resultant positive impact on your mind. For ultimately, *they are connected*.

Awareness is one of the key tools for unlocking your innate intuitive intelligence. Simply being aware of the things that are often hidden in us — be they buried traumas, signals from your body that you aren't conscious of or the things you unconsciously know and think — allows you to harness their powers and make changes. Doing so is but one of the first steps towards a better life, and health.

This is a holistic book, of which its sum is greater than its parts — each chapter will build upon those that came before it, instead of a mere smattering of separate lessons. And our bodies, similarly, are no different. You are made up of cells; those cells group together to form tissues; tissues group to form organs; organs group to form a system, and finally the integrated system forms *you*!

Throughout, you will learn about the importance of health, the mind/body relationship, where emotional trauma comes from, how to be more understanding of yourself and how to listen to your body. This will allow you to craft a personalised way to apply this knowledge, in order to consistently and sustainably improve your health.

Following this book step by step will enable the understanding necessary to rediscover yourself, building a platform through which to achieve the physical results you desire without the need for excessive effort.

You will find a variety of information and guidance in this book, yet this will not simply be in the form of abstract theory. Instead, I offer valuable advice that you can immediately put into action, in addition to various conceptual tools to allow you to better understand yourself and your health.

For now, let me give you a rundown on what to expect as you continue reading. The book will comprise three parts which, when combined, will provide you with all the resources necessary to start your journey. And as you wander through, you will find that each chapter also has action items you can implement right away, to build stackable progress as you journey towards greater health!

We'll begin by covering the fundamentals of health, and the conceptual tools required to move forward and implement this knowledge. In **Chapter 1**, this will include touching upon what exactly the entrepreneur's curse is, demonstrating the reasons underpinning why so many of us struggle with our health.

Chapter 2 will then provide an overview of what good health is, not merely incorporating simple rules such as 'eat vegetables', but rather helping you to understand the *fundamental nature* of good health.

This section will then lead into **Chapter 3**, introducing the P.F.A. approach, which encompasses the three most crucial components of achieving good health — *purifying, fortifying and amplifying* — while elaborating on some useful ways through which to conceptualise each of these.

Moving to **Part 2**, you will be introduced to the concept of working with your subconscious. Made up of six distinct chapters, this will provide you with the knowledge required to tap into and understand your subconscious, the psychological restraints holding you back and how to take action as you cast away these inhibitions. This will ultimately help you access the answers within you, and better understand yourself.

Chapter 4 will ask the question: are you wired for bad health. This will explore the importance of acknowledging that each of our minds have been hijacked, but that now is the time to change this programming.

Chapter 5 will expand upon this, introducing various ways to change your thought patterns, which in turn will allow you to better deal with cravings and negative thoughts.

Chapter 6 will establish the concept of your 'hidden iceberg', enabling you to better understand and access your subconscious thoughts and behaviours, in order to regain control of your thought processes and steer the ship towards a healthier future.

Moving, then, to visualising how to take more direct action, **Chapter 7** will show the path to making the *un*controllable, *controllable.* Built upon and furthering the concepts established prior, this chapter will continue to help you access and control your hidden subconscious signals and desires. This will allow you to better understand yourself, by directing your subconscious in accordance with your conscious desires.

Chapter 8 will then contribute the methods through which you can be right 100% of the time, based on both your innate intuitive intelligence and use of other critical techniques.

And finally, to conclude this section, **Chapter 9** will show you how to kill what I refer to as your 'mind worms' — the most effective ways to get rid of the buried memories and thoughts that hold us back.

As a culmination of all that it follows, the third and final **Part 3** will then provide you with clear and easy devices to start your health journey.

Chapter 10 will start by offering guidance on finding your own personal, optimum health plan.

This will lead into the 6-week challenge I will offer you guidance towards in **Chapter 11**, a simple and easy-to-implement plan that will allow you build sustainable action beyond simply reading this book.

And finally, **Chapter 12** will show you how to track these actions, to both sustain your motivation and realise the magnitude of your achievements.

All that is left now, is to just get started!

Part 1

The Secret Every Entrepreneur Needs to *Stay* Successful

Throughout this book, I will explain what makes good health, and the things needed to achieve it. That being said, unlike many health books that suggest that they can provide you with some fad diet or 'secret' evidence only they claim to know, I want you to listen to the person that knows you best: *yourself*.

In this first section, the problem I am certain you face will be explained — how to build a business and amass financial wealth while keeping, or even improving, your health. This will allow you to conceive of health in an entirely new way.

So, if you're ready to start that journey to progress toward exponentially better health, then read on.

Chapter 1

What is The Entrepreneur's Curse?

Throughout this chapter, I will explain why many entrepreneurs often struggle with their health, leading to what I deem their *curse,* some factors of which I am sure will remind you of yourself.

To start, take a few moments and ponder these questions:

- Are you healthy?
- What actions led you to your current level of health?
- Do you think the steps that got you here have helped or harmed your health?

Entrepreneurs can be a variety of different people, from a variety of different backgrounds, each with their own individual goals. However, your similarities manifest in a shared drive to make a large impact, and to succeed in your vision. You sacrifice in the name of this vision, push yourself and inspire those willing to listen to go where others do not even dare. You work for hours or even days at a time, without food or rest. You prioritise your vision above all else. You sacrifice everything in the name of business success and will take one for the team every single time. What's more, you take all the responsibility. *"If it's going to be, it's up to me"*, right?

You have worked hard, faced a lot of stress, and never really stopped for a moment. Now, this mindset can be great for your business vision. Yet as someone who was in your shoes, and who has worked with many, many entrepreneurs, I can safely say it is unfortunately a mindset that is not good.

Now, I am not just talking about *physical* health here. Your emotional well-being may also be at risk, as well as your *mental* health. As an entrepreneur or busy executive, you constantly have to put out fires, and prioritise what to do in order to make sure that the business stays successful. And in doing so, you often don't take time to deal with some of the strong emotions that are invoked when putting out those fires. This is where they can accumulate, and cause problems over time.

Now, if this happens once, we can most likely handle that. But when this accumulates over the years, you will slowly, little by little, run yourself into trouble. And when you are mentally unwell, due to the burying of a haul of uncomfortable emotions, both your body and mind will suffer. This is the *Entrepreneur's Curse* — the drive that makes you succeed is the same drive that harms your health, as you continuously strive to solve problems without actually dealing with the emotions behind them.

Entrepreneurs always hear a lot of statements and absorb ideas like, "Sleep when you're dead," or, "Always be hustling." You have associated never stopping with success. You think that if you stop for too long, or give yourself a break, that somehow you will fail. Now, this is not a judgement. I know this drive to succeed, and it is what has got both you and I to where we are. Along with this drive, you will also likely, and subconsciously, have learnt to crave stress. You may feel that if you are not stressed, you are also not performing or working hard enough. You might associate the stress you feel on a daily basis with the success you have achieved, to the point where you cannot conceive of such success without constant stress. It is almost as though your body is so used to the stress that you don't know if you could function without it.

Yet this drive to always be working, consumed by your business, and to be stressed while doing it, is simply not sustainable. If you continue down this path, *something will break*. If you do ever stop, perhaps you feel unequipped to handle it. But, if you don't, you may well die a lot earlier than you should. And I'm pretty sure you don't want that.

Let me use an analogy to better explain this. Imagine that you have a horse; you learn that if you hit the horse as you ride it, it will go faster. So, indeed, you hit the horse when you want it to go faster. But what happens if you keep on flogging the horse, day after day, hour after hour, minute after minute? It doesn't take a genius to figure out that, eventually, it will collapse.

This is like the stress that drives you. It is the short-term impulse to go fast, but eventually, going at this speed, and being 'flogged' on an ongoing basis, will hurt and likely lead you to an early demise.

If the above resonates with you, may I suggest a moment of reflection, in order to instigate a radical shift in your perspective. To put it simply, *your success is not worth the price of your health.*

In addition, there is another way to understand the Entrepreneur's Curse. You have perhaps heard the saying 'be like water'? This was a favourite of mine growing up. The way I interpreted this was to use the energy of what is around you to go with the flow, and not go against the natural flow of life. By doing so, you can be more powerful than you ever thought possible.

Think about how powerful water is. When you wash your face, you splash water, and it washes dirt off. Now, if I told you water could wash your face off, you'd probably think I'm crazy. But isn't that what the waves of the ocean do when they beat up against the cliff of a mountain? What happens over time? That's right, the water carves into the rock face and erodes away some of the hardest substances in the world.

Now, imagine you are a water droplet, as part of a stream, and you want to go to the top of a mountain. You cannot reach the summit by going back up the stream, because the water is flowing one way. Indeed, it would be impossible for water to defy gravity.

However, you can get to the top if you follow the water. You simply flow downstream, reach the ocean, change states by evaporating, before finally raining down on the mountain top as a raindrop. By going with the flow, you can achieve your goal. Granted, it does take working in flow with other water droplets, changing states from liquid to vapour, and back to liquid, but those are lessons that are yet to come.

This very attitude, of simply going with the flow, can be applied to most areas of life. You, as an entrepreneur, have goals. You consider yourself an independent person, and often put your energy in a particular direction. This has got you somewhere, but usually at the expense of other areas of your life. And the longer you live, the harder it gets. You can only defy the natural flow of life for so long.

Now, going with the flow does not mean to give up, or stop trying. In fact, going with the flow — to be like water, and not waste a lot of energy while stubbornly trying to stay the same — is actually the best way to reach the goals that you set for yourself.

You reach the top of the mountain this way: not by defying nature, but by *becoming one* with it. Things change, and you need to change with them. Just like how water changes to vapour to then ascend to the clouds, you too need to change in order to reach your new goals.

The law of nature is that what stagnates, decays. This ultimately means that *if you don't use it, you'll lose it,* a simple notion that is applicable to health and almost every other area of life.

You cannot achieve your goals unless you put in energy. But what if the very energy you are putting in is in the wrong direction? That would be the ultimate waste of time, doing something well that need not be done at all. Instead of pushing, what if you were strategic, and placed yourself in a position where you are pulled towards success? Just like water flowing downstream. When aligning with such a current, you can achieve better success, better health and a better life, with close to no effort.

Now, for a moment, I want you to ask yourself once again: why did I pick up this book? I bet it's because something feels off, that something isn't right with your health.

Perhaps you are now feeling more and more tired? Maybe you are feeling like you're approaching a breakdown? Or you just know something isn't right with your health, but you cannot pinpoint it?

Are you wondering to yourself how long your body will hold out, or if it even *will* hold out, until you reach your goal? Or maybe the success that came so easy earlier in your journey is becoming harder and harder to come by? Maybe you just sense that your work and everything else in life is off balance. These thoughts, this growing awareness, is your subconscious trying to tell you something. We all have a subconscious and a conscious. The former is, essentially, an intelligent part of you that is underneath your conscious awareness, hence its rather telling name: *sub*conscious.

One important thing to note is that your subconscious is NOT stupid. It knows that if you continue doing what you're doing, you will struggle. The subconscious is only focused on one thing, and that is getting you to function optimally. It does so by continually sending out subtle signals to get your attention.

By identifying these signals, and listening to them, you will come to learn a lot about yourself. But more importantly, you are going to unequivocally know that your subconscious is a powerful ally, fighting by your side to help you achieve the goals you want.

The trouble is the subconscious rarely speaks directly; it is a little mysterious and likes to instead speak with emotions and mental imagery. First, you have to learn to identify these signals, before then responding to them. Understand that both your body and mind are amazing, and that you can adapt and change, no matter what condition you are in.

I will often talk about my patients in this book, because they are my greatest teachers. For example, when patients join my course, they often have no idea what exactly is wrong. Instead, they just have a feeling that something is off. Their blood work might be pristine, but somewhere in the back of their mind is that little voice egging them on to find answers. The amazing thing, however, is that they *do* know something is wrong, which is why they sought me out. I believe that you are here because of the exact same reason. You have a sense that, if you don't make a change now, there could be problems down the road.

This feeling is an indication that you are, in fact, suffering from the Entrepreneurs' Curse. You have achieved success at the expense of your health. Yet now is the time to change this, in order to achieve even greater, more durable, success, both in business and in life.

Yet how can you listen to your subconscious, and know what it is telling you, in order to achieve this? How can you know if it is telling you that your health is getting worse? Let's start exploring together.

Listening to Your Subconscious

Understanding the subconscious is crucial in your journey to achieving good health. The root cause of your behaviours, of your patterns, of everything, rests upon the rules of life that you have learned subconsciously, going all the way back to childhood. We are all a combination of both our parents and our environment.

Everything we do, from how and what you eat, to how you handle stress, comes from learning and mimicking.

We have all had conscious and subconscious thoughts from when we were young, and these affect us in subtle and almost imperceptible ways. What's more, these effects can be a major cause of our health problems. Now, this does not merely regard physical health in the classic sense, but your emotions too, which are now being recognised as almost more important than the physical aspects of health.

I focus a lot on the mind in this book, because it's the real reason behind poor health. Yet everything in your mind is within your control, and you can change it. Even the act of reading this at this very moment, in a sense, is the beginning of this change. The challenge before you, now, is getting in touch with yourself, understanding what is inside of you before then making sustainable changes.

You can start right this moment, with an exercise to get in touch with your subconscious self. If you look deep inside, who knows the answers you will find!

Why do this? Because when you can see what is within you, important and relevant answers to your questions start to surface.

An exercise is provided below, and to follow along get a pen and paper in preparation to take notes.

Ready? Get started.

Here's the link if you like to be guided through your Getting Unstuck Meditation: https://youtu.be/AWo0X9T6NAA

Have both your feet planted firmly on the ground.

Notice how well supported your feet are by the floor. Sit here comfortably for a few seconds.

Take a deep breath and notice how the breath enters your body. Notice how your lungs expand and fill with oxygen.

As you breathe out, notice the movement of air exiting your lungs, washing out the carbon dioxide from within them.

As you become more and more comfortable, allow your eyes to gently close.

As your eyes rest, place one hand over your heart. Imagine it expanding… and breathe in slowly for the count of six seconds.

As you breathe in, imagine your heart expanding and becoming larger. Fill this heart space with the feeling of gratitude.

Now, as you breathe out for the count, again, of six seconds, allow your heart to contract and shrink. While it is becoming smaller, imagine that it is squeezing every unsupportive emotion out of the body. Any tension, worry, fear, shame, doubt. Any negative emotions that are holding your back.

Take another deep breath in. Feel the heart expand, and fill it up with the feelings of gratitude.

As you breathe out, allow all tension to leave your body from your heart, emptying yourself of emotions that do not serve you.

Let's take another two breaths here. Breathing in, 2,3,4,5 and 5.

Breathing out, 2,3,4,5 and 5. Notice how your feelings and thoughts start to quiet down.
Let them just "be there"

If any images flash up to the screen of your mind, just allow them to move across the screen and observe them impartially.

Allow them to come to rest within yourself.

In this state, ask yourself:

- *"Where am I now in life?"*

Notice what comes up for you. It could be colours, shapes, symbols, or perhaps a memory will start playing back. Whatever comes up, gently open your eyes and take down a few notes.

Once you are done with the notes, have your eyes gently close and return to the breath.

Allow your heart to fill up with the feelings of gratitude.

As you breathe out, allow your breath to empty you of any negativity.

Now ask yourself:

- *"What is emerging in my life, what is next?"*

And finally ask yourself:

- *"What is the obstacle in my life?"*

As your subconscious provides you with answers to the third question, jot them down on your paper.

Take a moment to review the answers that have come through to you.

What have you written down? Are any of the answers surprising? How do they sit with you?

Congratulations!

You have just practised communicating with the deeper parts of yourself. Keep the paper with your answers with you for the next week, and keep thinking about them. Notice how the answers evolve and gain meaning.

As you add to the insights gained,
you will come to clearly know that
all the answers you need are already within you.

And now, I am pleased to say that you have learnt about the very meaning of The Entrepreneur's Curse. However, awareness is only the beginning of the journey.

The next section has some specific questions you can get started with, so you can begin to reflect on your health and how to improve it. Take time to go through each of these, while utilising the accompanying video in the action items attached next, that will guide you through them.

Action Items 1

These first action items are intended simply as a matter of reflection.

Ask yourself:

1. **Are you healthy?**
2. **What is not perfect yet?**
3. **What next step will help you in this journey?**

Remember, this is the very start of your health journey.

4. **What has made you successful?**
5. **What has gotten in your way?**
6. **What needs to change?**

Start inspecting yourself and your behaviours, while identifying the roadblocks that you face.

Practise the breathing technique and connecting with your subconscious mind. As you become proficient at this, you will build a skill that you can use for any part of your life.

After you consider these items, I invite you to move onto the next chapter, and find out just *what makes good health.*

Chapter 2

What is Good Health?

This chapter will provide an overview of what good health is, not merely incorporating simple rules such as 'eat vegetables', but rather helping you to understand the *fundamental nature* of good health. By now, I hope the importance of better health is clear, and that the lack thereof ultimately is or will be an obstacle. In addition, you should now be beginning to understand that your subconscious is pretty powerful. So, in order to improve your health, where do you begin?

To understand how to enact such improvements, we first need to understand what health is. To start off, consider this: what are you made up of? If you answered cells, you are absolutely right. Although, technically, we are made up of different particles, such as atoms, which vibrate at different frequencies. These particles combine to form elements, like hydrogen and oxygen, which then aggregate together and become molecules, for example amino acids. These molecules interact and combine to become carbohydrates, fats, proteins or DNA/RNA, the combination of which finally form our cellular structures.

The takeaway? We are electromagnetically powered cellular organisms. Since cells make up the basic subunit of the body, does it not follow that, if your cells are healthy, then you in turn will be also? This line of inquiry thus indicates the importance of finding an answer to the question: what factors make up cellular health. Luckily, this is one that is surprisingly simple.

So, what does it take for a cell to be healthy? It needs to breathe, drink, eat and get rid of waste. *That's it.*

Taking that logic, your health has four simple components:

1. **The air you breathe**
2. **The water you drink**
3. **The nutrients you ingest**
4. **The waste you remove**

Is any of this really a surprise?

Some people may try to give you overly complicated answers. But at the end of the day, the answer is straightforward. To be healthy, we need to breathe good air, drink clean water, and eat nutritious food. Then we need to remove waste.

So, the same things that support a healthy cell are naturally going to support a healthy human being, a notion that is crucial. Each of us have around 70-100 trillion cells that make up our bodies. Our cells group together to form tissues; tissues with similar functions form an organ; organs with similar functions form a system. Combine all these systems together, and you get a human being. Ultimately, all you must do is look at how to support your cells, and that will lead to you becoming healthy as a whole.

All of the health we need is contained in our cells, and when we create an environment that supports healthy cells, we thus create a healthy human. Health is an inside-first approach. Remembering this, will serve you well as you head into the future. For now, let me introduce you to a real-life scenario that highlights the importance of cellular health; enter GP6D deficiency.

GP6D deficiency is a genetic disorder whereby the body does not have enough of an enzyme called glucose-G-phosphate dehydrogenase (namely abbreviated to GP6D). This enzyme is, crucially, important in protecting red blood cells.

Children who have this genetic disorder have:

- Pale skin
- Persistent and / or severe tiredness
- Dark coloured urine
- Yellow skin or eyes

A lack of G6PD leads to red blood cells breaking down too easily when a person is exposed to certain foods, viruses or medications.

There is no cure for G6PD deficiency, and it is a lifelong condition. However, most people with it have a completely normal life, as long as they avoid the triggers. When you avoid things that damage the cell, the body remains healthy. There are various other examples where people cannot process certain chemicals, due to the fact that they lack other enzymes. Again, if the cellular health is taken care of, there is no detrimental effect to the body.

To sum up, you may add things like supplements to your diet or try to fix some things about your lifestyle, but if you don't focus on improving your internal health, by providing air, water and food to your cells, it will all be in vain. Even if you add some extra fruit into your diet, but still chain-smoke and don't drink enough water, you will not improve your health. Everything has to be done from the *ground up.*

This is to say that you have to create a *cellular* environment from the ground up, one that is conducive to health, while supporting the cell in its entirety. Merely adding one or two things alone isn't going to help. No, for sustainable health, you instead need to implement a complete and holistic solution.

Remember the 13-year-old girl mentioned in my letter to you, who was diagnosed with bone cancer? Originally, she actually came in with something wrong with her leg, for which we investigated and identified the problem, before she then went to a specialist for treatment. She came back after six months telling us she had started on chemo and radiotherapy, and for a while, things seemed to be going well. But when they did a scan of her lungs, she was told that the cancer had spread throughout her body. This forced the treating team to change the chemo regime, which initially slowed the spread. But after some time and a second scan later, the cancer continued to march on.

The advice, at the time, from the treating team was to repeat the chemo. I said to her, "I get what you're going through is really tough — I wouldn't wish it on anybody. But if a treatment doesn't work the first time, does it make sense to keep doing what doesn't work? You need a different treatment plan." Following our discussions, she and I started working together, where we focused on a holistic daily plan of drinking, eating and breathing well. The goal was simply to provide the cells with an environment that they could thrive in, instead of focusing on treating the cancer.

The logic was that if the cells were strong, the body would be strong, and the cancer would be thus cleared by the body itself. Within a couple of months, the treating oncology team saw the positive results, as her scans showed that the cancer had stabilised. After six months, the nodules on the CT scan had calcified (i.e., the body had completely encased and isolated the cancer). The treating team were overjoyed, yet merely chalked her cancer cure down to a miracle.

Quite amazingly, none of the doctors, nurses or treating team were curious or even open to knowing what she had done to alter her condition. To them, her miraculous recovery was simply that: a miracle.

There are three main lessons to take from this story. The first: health is cellular. Creating the conditions for healthy cells will lead to one's whole being becoming healthy. In these types of cases, it is important to understand that cancer is not the natural state of the body. We know scientifically that cancer cells exist in everyone, but that the healthy internal cellular environment allows our bodies to clear these cancer cells. It is only when the cells are unhealthy that they stop doing their normal jobs, which can then lead to a toxic internal environment in which a cancer can survive. So, realise that no matter how bad your health is right now, making changes to improve your cellular health will go a long way to improving your overall health. The answer is to start working from the *inside out,* and from the *cells up.*

The second takeaway from the story is that focusing on these small simple steps can go a long way to improving your health; it does not always require fancy or drastic actions.

For example, no matter what lifestyle you have right now, if you were to simply swap one canned drink for water, or one of your takeaway meals for a healthy meal, or in fact do just two more minutes of physical activity every day, each of these would be an effective start. And then you can try to do another small step, building these up until they become habits that occur automatically. I will teach you how you can create new habits almost effortlessly in more detail later. But for now, simply know that you do not need some magic supplement, crazy diet or insane exercise regime that will completely exhaust you. You can start today with small steps to create this healthy, positive cellular environment, and your health *will* improve.

The third and final point of this story is to believe in, trust and work with *yourself.* My patient left her health decisions to the treating team out of fear. It was only after everything had failed and she was told to make a wish list and start ticking them off that she decided to change track. It was her self-belief that a cure was possible that gave her the courage and conviction to move forwards and allow her body to heal.

I never claim to know what is best for your health; only you have that power. My job is simply to help you understand what is uniquely good for you, and for you to use that knowledge to better your health. However, what you also need to understand is that creating a good environment inside you, one that is good for your cells, is how to achieve sustainable health improvements.

A lot of people ask themselves, "What do I need to do to get healthy?" And then their mind tries to answer, "Oh, you could try some protein supplements, increase your vitamin intake, do cardio training or yoga, cut out carbohydrates." But for every piece of 'health advice' you will ever hear, there will always be someone singing from a different hymn book and giving the exact opposite advice! I'm sure you have heard many ideas on how to be healthy, what to eat, what kind and amount of exercise is best, and so on.

And guess what? **They all WORK!**

Yet only to a *certain* extent, varying across *different* people.

That is why no matter what diet, what supplement, what exercise program, there is always a wide array of positive testimonials for each, because different people respond to different things. Have you ever seen one person's testimonial come up for twenty different supplement regimes and exercise programs? I seriously doubt it — but why? Because once you find your sweet spot and know how to get healthy based on your body's own unique needs, you don't need a ton of different programs, you can instead just do your own.

From here, the question that arises is how do you know what is or isn't good for your cells and your health? The answers are simple. In fact, the answers are inside you, yet you have simply lost touch with your inner self. For now, all you need to do is provide your cells with fresh air, clean water and nutritious food. That is the start. Doesn't it seem obvious? That is because you knew this!

Our Ephemeral Needs

It is worth recognising that you have more than just physical needs to be healthy, because everything within you, mind, or body, is interlinked. If you feel depressed, it is hard to motivate yourself to enact a healthier lifestyle. You are likely going to struggle to be active or eat right when you are in such an unresourceful emotional state. And if you're unable to do anything but stay in bed, it is unlikely that you'd have the energy to prepare a nutritious meal or get up and exercise, or even breathe deeply.

We all have finite amounts of energy, yet everything (and I mean *everything*) requires it. Whether it be staying in bed or out running in the park, different actions require different amounts of energy. The thing is, every ounce of your energy expenditure is accounted for by the body. Feeling emotionally drained? That is not just an expression, it is literally a drain of energy. Have that incessant mental chatter that you just can't get rid of? That's consuming energy. Disharmonious relationships: draining energy.

Being happy requires energy too, but unlike unresourceful emotions, true happiness provides more than it takes, so you get a surplus. To sum all of this up; your mood affects your motivation; your motivation affects your actions; your actions affect your physical well-being. The opposite is also true, as your physical interactions can both directly and indirectly affect your mood.

Here is a simple example: if you eat a lot of junk food, you are likely to experience both sugar highs and sugar crashes, which can manifest as being tired a lot of the time. If you fill your body with unhealthy substances, such as those contained within junk food, your mood will respond negatively to the imbalance caused by the various chemicals. This, in turn, can affect your physical health, leading to the formation of a downward spiral.

The important thing to note here is that there are needs beyond the physical which can affect our health. By being mindful of them, we can start down the track of providing our body with the right components for healthy cells. This is because the body affects the mind, and the mind in turn affects the body.

Tony Robbins, the author, life coach and philanthropist (to name just a few of his engagements), uses the 'Six Human Needs Model'. This model dictates that, for human beings to survive and thrive, all six of the following needs have to be met:

- Certainty
- Uncertainty
- Significance
- Love
- Growth
- Contribution

The first four are survival needs, and most people will go to great lengths to secure these. Having the certainty, for example, that when you wake up the roof won't fall on your head, and that you will be safe, is something we all generally crave. Now, of course, if there is absolute certainty and no variety in your life, that would be boring, because there would be no surprise and excitement. Yet a completely uncertain life can be chaotic, and impossible to build routines or plans around. Therefore, we need a degree of certainty, but we also need a healthy dose of uncertainty / variety to balance it out.

Significance, on the other hand, relates to the need of feeling that you matter. Everyone wants to feel that way, and will try to find all kinds of avenues to do so. Without a sense of significance in the world, we tend to regress inwards and become withdrawn, since nothing we do matters.

The next need, 'love and connection', is about having relationships with other humans. Indeed, we are ultimately social creatures. Therefore, even if you are very introverted, in order to be happy, you do need some interactions and relationships with other people.

The last two needs are growth and connection. Now, these are not survival needs. Instead, they are related to a higher sense of self, a higher purpose, to our spirit, if you will. We want to feel that this higher aspect of ourselves connects with us and can connect with others. We want a sense that we are moving forward in life, that we are growing, and that we contribute something in some way. And while we could live without this, it really is a need people require in order to thrive.

So, what does any of this have to do with health?

Well, the first relation is that having a model can be used to help you better understand yourself. Secondly, you need to align your health goals with your human needs for them to be *effortless,* and more importantly *sustainable*. It isn't enough to just think, "I'm gonna eat more vegetables." You also need to consider how your needs are being met *by* eating more vegetables, for example by lowering your blood pressure, or lowering the risk of digestive problems.

As you reflect upon this information, I hope it has allowed you to appreciate how important it is to match your goals to your needs. Now, if you sacrifice these needs in the name of health, it is likely that you won't actually be happy *or* healthy. Yet if you can find ways to satisfy these needs *and* link them to your health goals, you will be able to achieve sustainable health. For example, taking up a sport that gives you a social experience may be better than exercising at home, as it satisfies the need for connection. It is of course important to remember that every person is different, so I cannot tell you which needs you should prioritise. Instead, my aim is to help you consider your own underlying needs, and their relation to your pursuit of health.

Finding the Answer Within You

As I am sure you have become aware, I have now mentioned a few times how you can find answers within yourself. In the previous chapter, an attempt was made to allow you to get in touch with your subconscious. And as you explore the book further, we will dive deeper into this process, allowing you to consult with yourself and get back in touch with your innate intelligence. For now, however, I will start by introducing a short and easy way to find the answers within yourself, that will allow you to improve your health.

One of the most effective ways to think about health, and find the answer within you, is through the principle of inversion, which refers to focusing on the opposite of what you want or should do.

By doing this, you can start to look into your own mind to find the answers you seek. This method is effective as it allows you to narrow down the options that can come to mind when you face a decision or are unsure of what to do.

Let's start with something simple. If I asked you right now what you want to eat, you might think of twenty different options and feel unable to pick. But, if I asked you what you *don't* want to eat, it is likely that you could specifically identify a few things. Using this thought process as a guide, you could then narrow down further, and eventually land quicker on what you *do* want, by immediately taking away from and specifying your few options. We can also bring this notion to the topic of health. Instead of looking for the answers to what makes you healthy, inversion asks, "What can I do to ruin my health today?" A question to which your mind can immediately respond with the answers.

Do it now. Ask yourself, "What can I do to ruin my health today?" Make a note of your ideas, and when you've finished come back.

While you were gone, I assumed you thought of some answers like the following:

- I can drink fizzy drinks over water all day
- I can have KFC, Hungry Jacks, or any other type of fast or unhealthy food
- I can lay on the couch and not do any exercise

If you thought of any of these, or any other notion that seemed overwhelmingly obvious, you clearly have some answers regarding the things you can do to make your health worse. At the very least, this line of thinking will provide you with an idea of what to avoid. Now, all you need to do is focus your efforts on avoiding these obstacles to good health, for as long as you can. This might seem a daunting task, but it is easier than you will be thinking right now, *trust me*. I say this as someone who used to keep shelves full of chocolate!

Your mind automatically knows all these things that could harm you, intrinsically providing us with answers to the question as to what makes us healthier. You can now say, "If I just avoid all those things, then I'll already be healthier." If drinking fizzy drinks all day, or eating fast food, or not exercising, are all obviously bad, it is just as easy to imagine some healthier options, right?

When utilising this thought process, our brains are able to highlight the different things that our minds think of, and we can use this information to then identify the gaps. You can then assess, "Okay, I do have a lot of information on what is both good and bad for my health — but there are still some things missing."

To explain a bit more about filling these gaps, you may right now think, "Well, I know that a home-cooked meal is better than McDonald's, but still, I don't know what the healthiest thing I can cook at home is." This is okay, we will work on that and you will be able to fill in these gaps. The principle of inversion can again be used here. For example, consider the question, "What ingredients would be the worst?" This is one that I know you would have the answers to, which you could then use to build a decent enough idea of what to cook with, and what to get next time you're at the supermarket. You won't be perfect to start with, and that's okay — it's a start!

This can also work for emotional distress. If you cannot think of how to feel better, you might at least know how to feel worse! And by identifying the things that can be most detrimental to your emotional distress, you can reverse engineer the actions to take moving forward by knowing the ones you should not.

Now, you may also think that by identifying the factors causing emotional harm, these will tell you what to avoid. Well, actually, no. Because hiding from emotions is not healthy.

A story that happened a short time ago with a client of mine demonstrates this particularly well. She had recently lost her dog to a car accident and was distraught. She didn't try to bury the emotion, she amplified it.

She started banging things and shouting at the top of her lungs, even taking her false teeth out so she could yell the way she wanted. Within fifteen minutes, she stopped. She was then able to refocus on being a loving mom to her kids because the emotion had gone through her instead of getting stuck or buried.

This is an example of how the principle of inversion can help speed up the emotional healing process.

It does so because you have to feel an emotion to move past it; you cannot simply block it. So, when you feel something negative, do not resort to this approach. Instead, think how you might be able to feel it to the maximum, which will allow you to find a way through. By exacerbating the feeling, you can then get past it, a concept we will go into more depth on in the next chapter. Yet for now, just make a mental note that, often, the way to deal with an emotion is not to work *through*, but instead by sitting with it, and feeling it fully.

Whether we are talking about choosing what to eat, what to do with your day or how to be both mentally and physically healthier, inversion is a great technique to get to the answer within you. You know what you need to learn, all the while having your own answer inside. Now you need only find it.

Throughout this book, I will frequently refer to the importance of internal, instead of external, answers. When we get sick or are afraid of a disease (as many have been over the last few years), we often look for some external solution. Or if we just want to improve our health through means such as losing weight or improving stamina, we turn to guidance from others.

However, so often the external advice we receive overwhelms and misdirects us. Or it offers only a marginal solution to a fundamental issue. I have already explained the three components necessary for good cellular health, and yet many so-called solutions and 'how-to' guides provide a quick fix, without fundamentally changing anything on a deeper level. But it does *not* work that way.

Now, I am not going to tell you that there is no use for doctors or medicine. But what I want to stress is that health is internal. You have to work to create a healthy body to deal with the threats that come to you. Taking endless supplements won't improve your health if you don't engage with any other important steps, because you have to build from the ground up. The answers to knowing how to improve your health cannot be found from anyone else. They are instead *within you,* this perhaps the most crucial concept to come away with when attempting to understand what you need to be healthy, not only in your body, but in your mind.

I hope you have now developed a better understanding of what good health is. Ultimately, I want you to find the answers. I hope that a lot of what I have said rings true, because you already knew it, or because you realised that you have been misdirected. My intention is not to overcomplicate things; I am simply talking about the reality that we need air, water and nutrition. Needs are things that you as an entrepreneur, along with everyone else, no doubt have. We all harbour those intangible needs, while we all of course want to achieve them. You now simply need to put in place the correct mentality in order to do so.

I hope that these concepts will allow you to take new steps on your journey towards good health. And to finish the chapter, let's hop right into some tangible actions you can take right now that will kick-start this journey.

Action Items 2

1. **Make a list of things you think are unhealthy. Then make a list of things you think are healthy.**

This will help you find the answers within you that you already know about what you should or shouldn't do.

2. **Think of your daily routine. How do the activities fulfil your needs? Make a note of the needs in relation to the activity.**

This can help you think about your lifestyle and work out what you need to maintain, adapt or consider with any changes.

3. **Practise Inversion to think about any situation.**

Don't think about the best solution, think of the worst. This will help you develop this skill, at which point you may find the answer right for you.

Chapter 3

P.F.A. Your Way to Exponential Health

This chapter will explain the three most crucial components of achieving good health, while elaborating on some useful ways through which to conceptualise it. This will allow you to understand some of the key concepts underpinning and outlined throughout the book, enabling a grasp on the nature of health, and its importance.

I have already established the different components of good health, and now we will turn to understanding the process itself that each of us must embark upon to become healthier. This will not be a series of compulsory steps dictating, "eat this, don't eat that," but will rather suggest the overall ongoing process we all need to follow to get to optimal health.

Again, this is not just about physical health, but also how to be healthier in your mind and your spirit as a result. By catering to both, you can achieve holistic and unified health goals, allowing you to succeed on a whole new level!

This chapter will allow you to gain an understanding of the process you must go through, and comprehend how some of the action items I suggest will specifically help you as an individual. Now, I do not recommend you try all of this advice immediately, by any means. You need to first view it as a whole, allowing you to then approach each part of the process in order.

The chapter will conclude with further action items to attempt in the meantime, while a lot of the advice will be directly relevant to the 6-week health plan you will find at the end of the book. As a result of this chapter, however, you will also be better equipped to see what your optimal health plan should look like, and you can aim for it. So, for now, you need to simply read on!

The process of health is broken into three components, which can be broken down further into three specific areas, where we have to **P.F.A.**:

- **Purify:**
  The Body
  The Mind
  The Spirit

- **Fortify:**
  Breathing
  Drinking
  Eating

- **Amplify:**
  Rituals
  Rhythms
  Routines

Tackling the first of these components, purifying is about getting the bad stuff out of you, and preparing your *body* to better deal with harmful things, such as the pollutants and toxins that can be found in the world around us (no matter how 'good' a lifestyle we live). It also is about having a better mental state, whereby a purification of the *mind* will allow you to better handle your surroundings. At the same time, a purified *spirit* is about directing ourselves towards a higher vision: our future, our big picture.

Fortifying is all about increasing the good stuff in our lives. This involves making sure we are consistently putting good things in our bodies and minds, and not slipping backwards. After you get rid of the bad stuff, you need to start putting the good stuff *in*, in order to fortify your health.

Amplifying is about maximising your healthy habits, and establishing a healthier lifestyle that will eventually become second nature. The difference between fortifying and amplifying is the difference between consciously and unconsciously being healthy.

Effectively, these all combine to ensure that you continue to put good stuff in and live a life that is oriented towards health without needing to think about it.

This is my overarching framework to achieve what I call exponential health. Later in the book, I will give you more explicit guidance on how to follow these steps in accordance with your own needs. But for now, I will explain a little about these processes and some of the basic things you will need to do to put this plan into place.

It may seem like a lot at first, and you may already be thinking, "Hey, this is all a bit much, I can't do this." Or, "What does all of this have to do with health?" But I assure you that it all connects. You will not be changing everything overnight; this book instead offers you step-by-step guidance to make incremental changes to your health. Everything you do will be easy, straightforward and most importantly, sustainable.

Also, being sceptical is hardly a bad thing. First of all, you will have heard so much in your life that was meant to be good for your health yet has turned out to be completely untrue. Truthfully, I would not be surprised if you *were* feeling sceptical. Second, scepticism means you are thinking, which is an indication that you are more likely to be aware of yourself and what will work.

Indeed, I want you to use this caution, but remember to keep an open mind, and your health in turn will thank you.

Now, let's dig deeper into the magic that is purifying, fortifying and amplifying.

Purifying the Body

We can best understand the notion of purifying by first considering it in relation to the body. When we ingest anything inside our bodies, it must first be broken down, before being assimilated, or in other words absorbed, into the body. Once it is assimilated, it can either be used or stored. In the case of a toxin, the body can't use it, so it has two choices, to store it or detoxify it. If your body has the required nutrients, detoxification is easy. But if you don't, then the toxin is stored temporarily until such time it can be detoxified.

The problem is that oftentimes the storage instead of being temporary, goes into deep storage. This is where the toxins move from superficial tissues to deep tissues and then finally get sequestered in either fat or stored inside bone. Then, as it's stored, the only way for it to be expelled is to first bring it up the storage chain until it is released and then it is able to detoxify it. This is why you need to detoxify: to purify your body. If we do not handle toxins, they build up and continue to accumulate, leading to the deterioration of our health.

It is important to understand a little more about toxins before moving forward. First of all, they can be a bit of a buzzword in health to mean all sorts of things; some people talk about detoxes where you stop eating a food item, and simply by doing so become fine. Yet toxins require very specific steps to be properly eliminated, which is not something that can be achieved *that* easily.

Toxins can be one of many harmful pollutants or even simple food items that your body is uniquely incapable of processing. For example, if you have severe reactions to wheat or dairy then these groups of items are toxic to you, even if you have eaten them your whole life. The bad news is that there is an inordinate amount of pollution in the world; the air we breathe, the water we drink and the food we eat have all been contaminated by toxins of various kinds.

A key point of consideration is that when you release toxins, your body needs enough antioxidants and nutrients to counteract them. Only when the toxins have been neutralised by these antioxidants and nutrients are they ready to be expelled from the body. This is where we sweat it out, pee it out or poo it out. Not glamorous, I know. So, purifying is as much about getting stuff out as it is preparing your body to be able to deal with toxicity.

Many people have toxins in them, even from birth, with research surrounding newborn umbilical cord blood highlighting this very pressing problem. There was a study by the Environmental Working Group examining this topic, by testing ten babies born in 2004. They found 287 chemicals in the umbilical cords, including Teflon, flame retardants, pesticides and other byproducts.

Now, on the one hand, these findings demonstrate how amazing our bodies are, through the notion that we can handle a lot of toxins and still carry out critical functions. However, while it is true that our bodies can function even with the presence of various toxins, the results also indicate the sheer magnitude we have to deal with, even from birth, which is not conducive to long-term health.

This constant presence of toxins means that we have to expel toxins that have been inherited from our mothers. These substances can poison us, leading to potentially significant health problems later in life. This is why we need to take the proper steps to remove these toxins that come from the world around us. Many of these toxins are stored in our body long- term, and are not things that can be expelled in a couple of days simply by using supplements. Instead they require sustainable and long-term changes in our health.

When your body has to deal with toxins, this function takes energy away from you, which can lead to fatigue. Every bit of energy used to remove toxins means less energy left over to deal with other processes in your body such as bolstering your immune system. This is why it is important to start from the ground up, by purifying your body first.

Purifying your body requires purifying your:

- Breathing
- Drinking
- Eating

It is via the air, water and food that toxins come into our bodies and threaten our health. We can encounter bacteria and viruses in the air when we come into contact with other people, car smoke, factories, cigarettes, fires and also pollen. In your home, you have dust mites, and pet dander if you have cats or dogs. There is constant contamination in the air around you, from multiple sources, all of which have a definitive impact on your health.

And yet we of course have to breathe all the time! Millions of people die every year from air pollution, particularly in developing countries where there are fewer regulations protecting air quality. However, no matter where you live, you need to purify the air around you to reduce the amount of toxins you breathe in.

Now, you may be thinking, what can I do? I live in a city, and I don't want to or cannot move. I understand. This is where nature truly shines, it has figured out the solution long before humans came onto the scene. One effective option is getting houseplants to purify your air. Now, there are many debates about what kind of plants are best, but any plant is better than none — a personal favourite of mine is the Mother-in-law Tongue. The name says it all!

Also consider using air purifiers to remove toxins from the air. International reports all agree that indoor air can be up to 5x more toxic that outdoor air. We won't go into the nitty gritty of these but suffice to say that an air purifier will serve you well many years into the future.

Next up for examination is your water.

Did you know that tap water has multiple contaminants in it? These range from heavy metals to persistent organic pollutants like pesticides and to pharmaceuticals like antidepressants, antibiotics and even cancer medications.

Your drinking water is rife with pollutants and worse yet, you are over 70% water and replenishing your internal body water is NOT optional! In addition, drinking liquids that are full of additives and chemicals will add even more harmful things into your body. The bottom line is that if you drink soft drinks (or other non-water beverages), you are failing to equip your body with the necessary ingredients to deal with the majority of toxins.

Proper hydration is key to dealing with the toxins we inevitably encounter

Detoxification is like cleaning the house floor. Even when you start with a clean bucket, full of soapy water, as you use the water it will eventually get dirty, and you will have to replace and replenish it. However, the problem is that many people don't add fresh water to their body; they just keep the dirty stuff swirling around.

The thing is, you can do all the other steps to detox your body, just like adding detergent to the bucket. But if you don't replenish the water, you won't get the results you want. This is why one key aspect of purifying your body is to drink plenty of good quality water, ideally filtered , which is one of the most powerful tools to remove toxins.

Food is our next main source of toxins. They can come in the form of metals like mercury in fish, chemicals put onto fruit and vegetables, or artificial cancer-causing colours, flavours and additives that line most supermarket shelves.

A key concept that I would like to impart to you is simply this, 'The earth is a closed system.' What that means is that what goes around comes around. We have the water cycle, the food cycle, the wind cycle. Every molecule on earth is recycled endlessly, moving from one organism to the next. So when we consider the whole ecosystem and state of pollution in the world, everything bioaccumulates upwards.

Small fish eat microplastics, the larger fish eat the small fish and we eat the larger fish. It goes on and on, and because we are at the top of the food chain, by default we consume animals or plants that are laden full of toxins as a result.

So how can we reduce the toxins in our diet? Well, a simple way is to eat SLOW foods. SLOW stands for seasonal, local, organic and whole foods. Basically, eat what grows from the ground or sea and nothing from a packet. Of course you are gonna need more discernment even with slow foods but this simple tweak in your diet would cut out a tremendous amount of manmade toxins in the food.

It is important to factor in other areas where toxins can affect us — medications, contraceptive pills, alcohol and recreational drugs can all have major effects on health, leading to an accumulation of a range of different chemicals in our bodies, which react in various ways.

We encounter a lot of these things at a younger age, while we are still developing, which can be extremely harmful. Issues for kids and teenagers can range from relatively minor physical reactions, such as rashes and other skin problems, to more severe respiratory issues.

Crucially, it is also important to understand that these toxins can also affect your mind. Therefore, the act of purifying your body actually ties into your mind, and even your spirit. Ultimately, if you have constant rashes, bloating, gas, pains or headaches, these can be from toxins in you.

Yet brain fog and an inability to concentrate can also be because your body is dealing with too many toxins.

When you start to understand the magnitude of toxicity that plagues the human race, is it no surprise that many people have niggly health issues like rashes, eczema, joint pain, insomnia, etc. from teenage years on. But just because you've been exposed to toxins your whole life, doesn't mean it is too late to do something about this.

We do not need to panic or be overly dramatic. In fact, the idea that you have survived despite the many harmful things you have had to battle shows just how resilient you are.

So, how can you go about properly and deeply detoxifying these toxins?

Well, there are two things that ultimately need to be done. The first is to reduce the number of toxins that come into our system. Now, I know you may not be able to simply go and live in the woods or remove all medications from your life. However, we all *can* take steps to reduce our intake of toxins as much as possible. The simple act of filtering our air and water, and eating SLOW foods is a great place to start.

Secondly, we need to equip our bodies with the nutrients and means to physically deal with these toxins properly. This all starts with the air, then water, then food. With proper breathing, hydration and food our bodies will be in their optimal state to handle the toxins we do encounter. It is essential that all the stages must be followed in the correct order and done at an appropriate speed. Why?

Many patients I see go all out, then they crash and burn. It looks something like this; cut out all sugar, refined carbohydrates, packaged foods, soda, wheat, dairy, nightshades, alcohol, smoking etc. It feels amazing for 2 days. Then they suffer withdrawal from the third, and by the end of the week it is all too hard, and they are back to status quo.

Instead, make change sustainable and long term.

Get to know the inner workings of your body. Imagine you have a blocked pipe — you can blow it up with dynamite, and have to repair the damage, or you can steadily drill it down using a fine bore, in order to get the flowing again.

Now, unfortunately for us, our 'pipes' run right back into us. Everything circulates and is connected to everything else. Therefore, we need to be equipped to deal with all the toxins around us. This is why it's important to do this in a particular order. Get stuff *out* first, and once you are purified, we can talk about what to add back *into* your body.

To get started on purifying, you will have to work on improving the air around you. Again, this could involve getting some plants around your home, while also spending as much time as possible in fresh, clean air. Next, you will need to work on purifying your water. Drink lots of it, and make sure it's properly filtered. These are easily implementable steps that anyone can get started with.

Start small. Work on creating
a better environment for yourself,
while enacting effective changes to your lifestyle.

Turning to food, we generally need to work on consuming natural ingredients — things that come from nature. However, there is something about food and purification that requires a bit more of an expansive explanation, that will allow you to work out what is good for *you*.

The Hourglass Model

The hourglass model is one that is beneficial to follow, both when it comes to purification and eating well. One of the main aims behind the model is to allow you to get to a baseline, a natural point of health, where you can automatically understand what is both good and bad for you. I can't tell you — no one can. It's your body. But you have to get to your own unique baseline to be able to understand what is good and bad. It's like resetting something to start over, to get back in touch with understanding your body and its signals.

So, look at this hourglass shape. This represents the diet. At the top of the hourglass, the widest part represents when you eat and drink whatever you want. The width corresponds to your diet's range, which is presumably where you are now. Then as you go down, the hourglass gets a little bit narrower. This means you need to take a narrower approach to what you eat, you remove one food item at a time. Just like real life hourglasses that have a set rhythm, we too cannot and do not rush down our dietary hourglass.

As you work our way down the hourglass the next day, the next week, your diet itself becomes a little bit narrower. This is where you could get rid of all red meats from your diet, for example. The week after, the hourglass gets even narrower, getting rid of all meats, perhaps. Then as you go down further, you are left with only fruits and vegetables, before finally reaching the middle of the hourglass, the thinnest part, where you are with only vegetables perhaps, not even fruits. And then coming out the other end, it gets thicker again, whereby we reverse the process and add foods back. Here, you add back the white meats, and/or you add back the red meats.

Now, we are not simply going through the hourglass with the intention of making no permanent change. The goal is effectively an elimination diet, where you get to see how different food items impact you. Each time you add something back, you see how your body reacts. Maybe you start to feel full of energy, or perhaps you feel more tired. Maybe your bowels react badly, or you have brain fog, or perhaps even the total opposite. From studying and feeling the impact, you will be able to understand what is good for you. Each time you eliminate or add something to your diet, notice how your body reacts. By doing this methodically, you will develop a keen sense on what your specific optimal diet would look like.

When you add back white meat, in this example, ask yourself, how has it made you feel? How does adding red meat feel? Maybe you don't want to add it back to your diet, because it feels heavy for hours post-eating.

> ***Pay attention, listen to your body and you will be amazed at how little dietary changes will dramatically impact your focus, energy levels, sex drive, sleep and any other area of health you care to explore.***

At the end of this you may find that there is a lot of food you don't like anymore, this is normal and an expected part of going through the hourglass. So many of us have gotten so used to eating highly processed sugary items sold to us as food but isn't *actually* food. You might enjoy the taste, and not question how it reacts with your body, for as far as you are aware that is how your body has always felt.

When you reset, you may notice foods you previously enjoyed taste horrible after reintroduction, because your body understands it's not good for you! For example, I often see that when my clients give up sugar for a while, they realise once they try them again that these treats taste sickly sweet, and fruit tastes a lot better. What's happening? Your body is learning to discern again. It is regaining sensitivity.

It's a little like being in a club with "doof doof" music playing. Initially it is loud, then your ear drums habituate. After you come out of the club you notice your hearing is down several notches but as you stay out in the quiet your ear drums reestablish their baseline and now you aren't shouting at the top of your lungs because you can hear again.

So, how do you start? Well, know this upfront, I do not, will not and cannot demand you cut everything out. Only you have the power to do that. Remember our conversation about going the whole hog and just jumping headfirst and cutting EVERYTHING out at once? Best not to do that.

Instead, I suggest you simply cut out red meat for one week, then white, then eat vegetarian for a week, and then live without dairy for a few days. Then cut out everything processed for a few days. Do the same for carbs, then fats, and then have a few days with just vegetables. Then you can reset and add things back in again, slowly.

Simple right?

Before we go any further, I have to bring your attention to one important concept. Your gut transit time.

Your gut transit time is simply how long it takes for food you eat to move from your mouth and come out the other end. This will allow you to identify the minimum duration of reactions within your body. For example, if your transit time is three days, and you eat eggplant on day one, it will be affecting you for three days at least.

As you pay attention to how foods affect your body you are going to start to make new connections. For example, you may drink milk and notice you have thicker mucus than normal. Now that you have drawn that link, you can decide if ingesting it is a good idea for your overall health.

As you get towards the narrower end of the hourglass your diet is going to be pretty bland. How long you spend at the most restrictive portion of the hourglass is individual. Some people do 1 week, others go for 3 months. The point is to assess how you feel when you are here. If it feels great and energy is overflowing within you and you have clarity of thought for the first time, then linger a little longer. Why cut short a good thing? — When you are ready, you can start adding food items back 1 item a week.

During this time, it is imperative that you really tune into how you feel as these are your body signals telling you which foods are helping vs harming your health.

It is highly likely that you will uncover allergies in this process that you had no idea about. Let me give you an example. I had a female client who was an aspiring actress, yet she had reached a point whereby her health was suffering. Then she got chronic fatigue. The reason was that she had wheat in her diet, in the form of granola bars — supposedly healthy bars that she was buying from health food shops! After employing the hourglass model, she had gone through the phase whereby she had cut everything processed out, was eating a very good natural food-based diet, not consuming anything that was packaged and was feeling great as her health was recovering. Soon after, however, as life got busy she forgot about the granola bar and it sneaked back into her life at one granola bar a week.

In the space of a month, her health started to re-deteriorate, because these bars were affecting her system that much. It was the wheat, ultimately, that was harming her. It wasn't until we were able to pick this up, and get rid of that component in her diet, that her health started to improve again. So, very small things can make a disproportionate amount of difference, particularly if your body is sensitive to them. Now can I guarantee you are going to have the same effect? No, but what I can tell you is that research from Harvard has shown definitively that wheat causes damage to everyone's gut irrespective of whether you have any symptoms. I am biased though because I keep seeing how elimination of this one food item changes lives.

I had an over 70-year-old on multiple morphine painkillers give away her walking stick and medications within the space of a month by eliminating wheat. I have a 40-year-old dear friend who kept having acne breakouts despite using hundreds of dollars of top line quality skin care products. The culprit...you guessed it. Wheat! These examples demonstrate well how the hourglass model allows us to identify items in our diet that are either causing us harm or benefits through the simple process of elimination and reintroduction.

Getting to your baseline through utilising the hourglass model allows you to get to a clean slate. This then allows you to determine what is good for you as you introduce different types of food. You will be amazed at how, after cutting food items out for a while, you react to it when you reintroduce them back to your diet. Your once-favourite snack could be the source of what ails you! The real question is: is there a better way of eating, to give yourself more energy, more vitality and less stress on your body?

The answer is a resounding YES!

What I can't do is provide you with the exact diet which will be fully optimised for you, but with the hourglass model you will discover it for yourself.

It is important to note that you should avoid artificial ingredients (a little more on that later as we discuss fortifying). Artificial ingredients are full of toxins, and your body is best at handling natural ingredients. Foods may disguise many unnatural ingredients, but if you really thought about it, you wouldn't want all the additives, chemicals and genetically modified organisms (GMOs) when you could pick, say, fresh fruit, veg, meat, fish and grains, that come from nature.

Once you know where your baseline is, where your body's natural sweet point is and where it reacts well to what you are putting inside your body, you can then start adding back the rest of the food groups that you previously eliminated and see how they affect you. Prioritising the 'natural' aspects of different foods will help you guide your decisions when eliminating and reintroducing types of food to your diet, combined with seeing how your body reacts from putting these decisions in place within the hourglass model, will effectively allow you to identify what is good for you.

At the same time, identifying what is bad for us is also crucial. For example, gluten. Some people clearly react badly to gluten and *do* know it is bad for them. Yet many are not aware of the negative effects it is having towards them. Many of my patients have noticed their skin gets considerably better when they cut out gluten, in addition to other positive effects.

What I recommend is, when employing the hourglass approach, to try eating food without gluten, and see how you react. If wheat-based products have no observable impact on your health, then it is fine to keep them. Yet if they cause a reaction in some way, cut them out. You can do this with many different foods, to work out what works for you. In combination with seeing what affects you negatively, you can then work out a diet that works for your own unique health. My more general advice, however, is that if you eat things with additives and chemicals, your body will most likely spend a lot of energy dealing with them.

Again, I am not asking you to cut out everything forever. It would be unsustainable to just eat vegetables all the time. But if you create a clean slate, purify and fortify your body, remove a lot of toxins from your system and begin to learn what your body reacts well to, then you will see clear improvement. It's a kind of reset, and a chance for you to understand yourself. So, don't panic! This is not forever. It's for data.

This baseline concept is an important part of this book. The baseline allows you to understand how *anything* affects your body. When you find this baseline of health, you can see how an activity, or a food item, reacts. You can listen to how your body responds and identify what works for you.

Now, it is important to remember that no two people will ever be the same. An awareness of this is crucial, as it will allow you to consider, internally, what you need for your own good health. This will then guide you in your decisions towards achieving optimal health. This is not something you will find immediately, but do not fret. We will continue to go through the steps that will allow you to get there as you read on, but never forget that this is what we are aiming for.

There is no one-size-fits-all approach. It is about finding that intuitive understanding of your own body, which is precisely why the hourglass model is so useful. It helps you escape external validation, allowing you to listen to what your body tells you, in order to comprehend what is healthy for you as an individual.

For the record, if you read something here and think, "This makes no sense," that is fine! I say the same thing to both those who do my course and are my patients. Ultimately, my aim is to allow you to understand your own body and look internally for the answers to find what is healthy for you as an individual. This is what I have dedicated my life towards, and everything I suggest is with this intention.

Now, this approach, rather than a strict diet, has a major advantage. Most diets are imposed on you externally by others. One person will exclaim, "Eat no carbs!" as another shouts, "Eat only fruit." But all of these contributions come from someone else's voice. Such external dietary guidance often seems stricter, and harder, to achieve, while facilitating no real comprehension of why the advice being given is actually beneficial. Yet, if you take the hourglass approach, you can find out for yourself what is good for you.

The benefit of this approach, as opposed to me saying, "Cut out x, y and z," is that by experiencing life without certain foods, and life with them added back, you can associate a negative feeling or negative taste with the things that you know are bad for you, but currently enjoy. Other diets just tell you to stop, but you feel you miss the sweet or cheesy or greasy taste of whatever it is you like that you know you shouldn't. However, when you cut it out for a while, before then re-adding it, there is a higher likelihood of you seeing that you actually don't *need* nor *want* it. This will enable long-term and sustainable adherence to a healthy diet, as you begin to no longer associate that particular food with pleasure.

This also works with the good foods that you normally avoid. You will begin to build new, positive associations with the foods that are good for and react positively within you as they are reintroduced. The greens that you've struggled to eat since your childhood will become an essential addition to any meal for you, and you will *want* to add them. I will expand upon the topic of associations again later, but for now I want to stress that if you feel scared to cut things out, don't panic! You will want to keep going with this process after seeing how you can live without certain foods, enabled via this model. You will realise that you feel better without the things you previously thought you relied upon — say red meat, processed cakes or whatever it may be — and have no interest in keeping them in your diet.

Additionally, because the aim is to find a good baseline, rather than trying to lose a certain amount of weight, you will be able to establish an internal goal. This is not one that merely concerns external validation of some arbitrary result that may not last. Instead, you should aim to find a sustainable lifestyle that you have an incentive to keep, as it has been discovered internally.

You must aim to build and sustain your own good health, not to hit this arbitrary goal. For when you aim for external validation, what often happens? So frequently, people go back to bad habits. Yet this model allows for sustainable good health, based on your internal motivation to achieve it.

Now, I hope you have built a solid understanding of the hourglass model. And even if you are feeling a little nervous about getting started, I hope you are interested to see the results. But as I said, we will start *slow* and *small*!

Now that we have discussed purifying the body, we must next turn to thinking about the mind, as you continue your purification journey while on the road to greater health.

Purifying the Mind
(and the Parasympathetic System)

Purifying the mind requires a similar approach to detoxifying the body. Bad things can creep in, whereby we need to handle and release them. Otherwise, they build up and our health can deteriorate. For example, if you are dealing with a lot of different emotional stresses, such as money troubles, relationship struggles or even worries about your sick pet, these can build up, just like toxins, and lead to a mental breakdown. So, we need to deal with them.

When encountering stress, each of us experiences an emotion of a particular kind, which is a fight, flight or freeze response. The different intensities of these feelings, naturally, require different responses. Yet if you don't release your pent-up feelings, your situation will get worse, or you will not be able to come to a more positive emotion. So, this is what we need to work on.

You have to feel emotions, as part of the process of purifying your mind. You can't simply ignore them. This will allow your emotions to be released, but just like with your body being equipped to deal with toxins, you need the mental 'nutrients' to address them. If you don't have these nutrients, then the emotions will rise back up, leading to the fight or flight response, which in turn will lead to more instability. This means that you need to equip yourself with the mental ability to address these emotions, otherwise you cannot purify your mind.

The graph below (Figure 1) will allow you to better understand these reactions, and how good health is related to the mind. Whenever anything happens to us, we can be present and engage with it, or we can be overwhelmed and freeze.

Our parasympathetic system reacts to events, which enables the 'fight, flight or freeze' response. This relates to our ability to deal with these emotions and events, which in turn relates to what we have learned subconsciously since childhood.

FIGURE 1

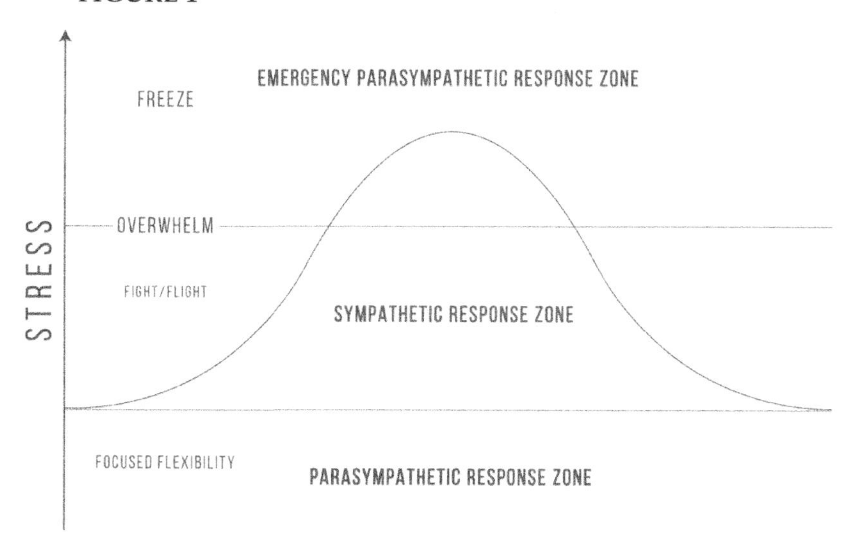

Contemporary scientific research, such as a recent study conducted by Lauri Nummenmaa and colleagues entitled 'Bodily Maps of Emotions', has begun to link emotions to various parts of the body. For example, when a person has a lot of anger, it tends to be related to the liver, while other body parts can signify different emotions, such as envy in the chest and head. We also know that when you have a deep tissue massage, there is a connection to certain areas that can release either memories or feelings.

The simple correlation is that our entire body is connected by the nervous system. Every single cell, every single tissue, has feedback that it gives to the central nervous system, the latter of which aggregates all of that data before deciding what to do with it. So, your health and body are linked with your emotions, while your emotions and mind are linked with your body. This is why we have to understand the mind and the body together.

FIGURE 2

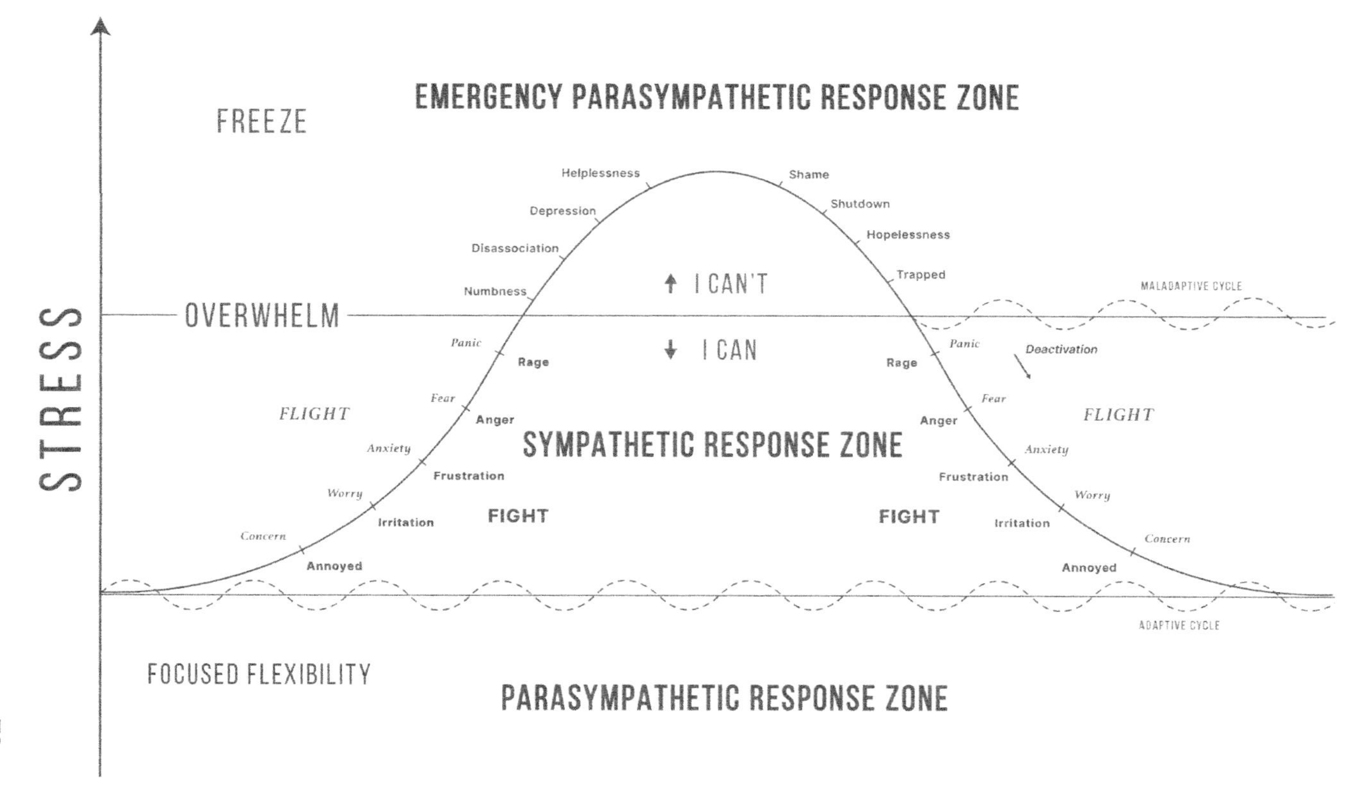

EMERGENCY PARASYMPATHETIC RESPONSE ZONE
FREEZE
STRESS
OVERWHELM
Helplessness
Depression
Disassociation
Numbness
Shame
Shutdown
Hopelessness
Trapped
I CAN'T
I CAN
MALADAPTIVE CYCLE
Panic
Rage
Fear
Anger
FLIGHT
Anxiety
Frustration
Worry
Irritation
FIGHT
Concern
Annoyed
SYMPATHETIC RESPONSE ZONE
Rage
Panic
Deactivation
Anger
Fear
FLIGHT
Frustration
Anxiety
Worry
FIGHT
Irritation
Concern
Annoyed
ADAPTIVE CYCLE
FOCUSED FLEXIBILITY
PARASYMPATHETIC RESPONSE ZONE

Now, look at the second graph (Figure 2), which shows different emotions, and more about the fight, flight or freeze response. Effectively, there is more stress the further along the curve you go. However, you must actually feel these emotions in order to then come back down.

For a moment, it is worth discussing stress in a way that you may find to be new. Stress is simply an increased level of arousal, which is something that you need a level of to engage with the world. Otherwise, you'd be asleep! However, when this arousal becomes more intense, you start to switch who you are into more negative emotions. Small incidents can build up, which you may consciously ignore, but your *body* will not. Instead, they can build up, before eventually, one day, you are in a sense of rage.

If we ignore one thing, then that is not going to get solved; it just sits there. But what happens when you start ignoring multiple, different things? This is where you can have constant fires and alarm bells, tipping the body into a state of being overwhelmed. And when you're overwhelmed, we then have to go through an 'emergency stop', so to speak.

The emergency parasympathetic nervous system kicks in and says, "Okay, we are now overwhelmed, so we're going to shut everything off." In this case, a person will become hopeless, helpless and emotionless, potentially falling into a deep depression. They will not be able to really feel anything, because they have gone over the threshold, thus then having the 'freeze' response.

Therefore, instead of being able to fight or flee, they will have gone so far that they become frozen. What happens is that the body simply locks all of that energy out, as when you experience an emotion so strong that it creates a muscular knot, it is frozen in place. But once you release it, it then goes away.

You can stay in this frozen state for a long time. Indeed, a lot of people do. You can look like you have adapted well but are instead actually internally numb and disassociated. In this state, you use a lot of energy, and will eventually crash.

This will affect all parts of your health, while killing your spirit because you deny feeling these emotions, which in turn can lead to burnout and meltdowns.

Perhaps this is what you are currently approaching? You can tell if you are in this zone by the variation of emotions you experience. So, again, try to be conscious of the emotions you feel. Do you feel a lot of emotions in a day, a week, a month? Do things just not phase you at all, even on an internal level? These could all be bad signs.

The thing about emotions, as they are being released, is that as you try to remove yourself from your frozen state you have to re-experience all of the different things that got you there. The illustration above in Figure 2 shows a curve going up, and on this curve are the different fight or flight responses. Whether you fight or you fly depends in part on your upbringing and how you have responded to different things throughout your life. And as you go past the threshold to the top emotions, you then go into freeze. Up at the top, you are frozen, but as you start to come down the line you start reacting again. The nervous system has to go back through the same pathways from which it came up.

The very bottom of the scale, when you come further down, is about being present in the moment, responding properly and healthily, and having the perspective to understand the reality of the things around you. This will allow you to better deal with stimuli. We will always encounter stress, and we will always react. You cannot escape a negative emotion, yet we can understand how to move past it, and get to what I call the 'adaptive cycle', which is when stimuli and your ability to cope with the stimuli are well matched and balanced.

This graph offers you a good way to recognise how you can deal with emotions. Look at how you are feeling — is it a fight, flight or freeze response? You need to be aware of these feelings, understand them and try to be present in the situation. If you realise you are feeling worried, then you may feel rage and freeze out. If you are in the higher emotions, you will need to come down and feel the next emotions in order to go through the fight and flight responses, before coming to a point where you are more present.

The key is that you have to actually feel these emotions, in order to work through them. However, the process of being aware of these emotions is crucial to overcoming them and being able to engage. You will then be able to work down through the various emotions, finish the cycle and be engaged with the situation, along with a crucial level of presence. Presence is all about awareness, being in the moment while clear on what surrounds you, and what is happening internally within you. This, ultimately, allows you to take more control.

The 'maladaptive cycle', on the other hand, occurs when you constantly remain in the negative emotions, and always use these as your stress response. But if you practise this process, deal with the emotions and feel them properly, you will be able to engage better with stimuli and the adaptive cycle. This, in turn, will allow you to deal with life better!

This sense of being present, of engaging with the world, is a way to be authentic and your true self, present in the moment while not focusing on worries about what *has* happened or what possibly *could* happen. When you are authentic, and everything you do acts in one direction which you decide, you will be synchronised, and have less friction within yourself. This will help your health, and help you direct yourself wherever it is you want to go.

For now, I want to make these cycles seem a bit more real to you. Imagine you started off your morning, for whatever reason, in fight mode — up in a panic, and feeling overwhelmed. In this case, you would have already crawled to the precipice of being either in the 'I can' or 'I can't' situations.

Whatever was happening at the time might have pushed you up into the freeze zone, forcing you to feel totally overwhelmed and helpless, with the need to call for help. To get to this stage whereby you are able to say, "Okay, I need to do something to change my physiology", this would be a way of starting down the activation scale. So, if you did call for help, you would then be able to manage the emotions. However, perhaps you still don't feel great, because you were experiencing some of these emotions as you were coming down through this very activation but managed to persist.

Then you chose to exercise, which stimulated your sympathetic nervous system and allowed you to come down this type of emotional ladder. As you came down the ladder, you activated your parasympathetic system by perhaps taking a shower, taking some time to yourself and then starting to connect with other people. Then you entered the adaptive cycle where you could be engaged and present for other people, because you now had a different perspective.

Simply being aware of your feelings is the best way to start, and you can do that *right now,* whenever you respond to something. Recognizing the emotions allows you to feel them, work through them and eventually be better able to deal with the world around you. This enables you to detoxify your mind, by equipping yourself to deal with these emotions as you release them.

You can stay in the adaptive cycle just as you can the maladaptive cycle. In order to stay in the adaptive range, you need to be aware, in order to then try to make it a habit. Try to feel the emotions, all the while aware of what you are feeling, and not bury them. Now, I cannot simply tell you, as an individual, how you can make it a habit. It is instead in your own hands to listen to your body. What I can offer is the first step, which is to build an awareness of your own body's signals.

Telling you about another patient of mine might also help you comprehend the maladaptive cycle. After a few weeks of working together, we came to understand that he was trapped in a cycle. What he would do was feel hopeless, go up along the curve, but then go down and deactivate. He was stuck in the maladaptive cycle. When he would go up, he would feel the emotions he didn't like, and then freeze. Then it would repeat.

To work through this, he had to accept that when he was going into a panic there would be fear, then anxiety, worry and concern. He actually felt he didn't want to see his psychologist because he wasn't feeling anything different. Yet because I explained to him this emotional slide, and tried to get him to feel these emotions, he began to feel new things besides hopelessness.

The fact he was able to feel anything else was a big shift for him; he was moving out of the freeze response, which is crucial when attempting to move toward the adaptive cycle. Indeed, you have to first *feel* through the hard emotions, in order to then get to the better ones. Do not ignore them, do not bury them. Feel them, amplify them and work through them.

When you get off the parasympathetic reactions, you will then go through the sympathetic reactions, which are very uncomfortable. This makes a lot of people stay in the same behaviour patterns, allowing them to avoid these feelings. This is why many entrepreneurs are trapped in this cycle - because they are used to the sense and pressure of having someone breathing down their neck.

I had one client, with whom I worked with for six months. I said to him that if he kept going the way he was, something would break. Well, it did. This forced him to slow down, yet when he did, he had no idea what to do with himself. He had no familiarity with rest.

This is something I touched on previously with you, as an entrepreneur; you are so used to stress, that you feel as though you cannot thrive without it! Yet when me and my client dug in deeper, and I explained how he was used to this high level of stress, he began to go, "Oh, that is crazy, I can't believe my mind has done this."

So, we worked on using stress as a resource to prevent his situation from happening again in a few months. The specifics that we focused on were setting up boundaries, and not taking on too many responsibilities. And to do that, we looked at his sleep. We ensured that he got more sleep than before and oriented all things around his sleep. He had to ensure he was back home on time to get the full amount of sleep, which allowed him to then regulate his behaviour. This led to him having less stress in his life, a change which not only had many positive individual results, but also those which trickled down towards his child's behaviour and relationship with his partner.

By identifying your emotions through placing them along the scale, you will be able to understand the necessity of feeling them. Too often we bury these emotions — yet, again, these can accumulate, causing deep unhappiness.

You can be free of these buried emotions,
if you simply allow yourself to pay attention
to them and feel them on a deeper level.
This will then allow you to have better health,
through which you can direct yourself more
effectively and efficiently towards your goals.

At this stage, you may be thinking that you can't deal with these emotions. That you aren't ready to face, say, your traumatic childhood, and that you just want to be healthier. Yet it is important to understand that everything is connected, a notion that we will engage with further throughout the book. Usually, we get uncomfortable when we tap into something true, or face something painful that is buried, which is normal. You can rest easy, however, as you will be guided with comfort and support through each integral step to battle these feelings. For now, though, use this graph to understand how your body and emotions are linked. Remember, it is your childhood that gave you the tools to deal with these emotions. Whether they are positive or not, is a challenge, and this is what we need to work on, for mastering such emotions is one of the most effective steps towards becoming both physically and mentally healthier.

Purifying the Spirit

Finally, we can come to the stage of purifying the spirit. What spirit means is more about your direction in life and the higher goals you set for yourself, rather than some vague concept or very specific and controversial idea. It is the higher self — what you want to become, your goals and your vision.

While often left unrecognised, spiritual health is important. For example, people who believe in a god or some higher purpose often feel a connection; they have a sense of something bigger than them. Putting time aside to reflect on this notion, whether through prayer or meditation, is a spiritual practice. At the same time, this higher power can also be something simpler. It could perhaps be your vision of the world, or even yourself. As far as I am concerned, being in touch with yourself, on a deeper level, and understanding who you are and what you want to do, is spiritual health.

There are a variety of spiritual exercises that you can use to engage with these ideas. As a brief sidenote, however, it is important to focus on these only after working on those for the body and mind. Things such as giving yourself some solitude, and a space to yourself, are really important. In this space, you can reflect, meditate, pray, or do whatever you want that you feel is a spiritual activity. Because ultimately, the goal is to think about something higher than yourself.

Now, this is of course a concept and engagement that is very subjective. Therefore, you can invert your thinking here. First, ask yourself: what is spiritual unhealthiness in your own mind? You may be able to better identify something here that is bad, to then go backwards, step by step, and work out what to you would be a spiritual practice, for you as an individual. It entirely depends on what you are connecting to. Are you connecting to your higher self? A god? Something else? For now, just reflect on this. It is essential to understand that your spirit is connected to your mind and body. If your body and mind are toxified, your spirit will be weighed down, restricting you from going in the direction that you want. Yet if you can work on purifying your mind and body, your spirit will be able to go where it wants. Indeed, you yourself can go where you want if you purify all parts of your body and mind.

Your spirit is your main vision of what you want to be, and where you want to go. And to have a pure spirit, we need a pure body and mind to synchronise all parts of ourselves.

Fortifying Your Breath

After establishing the importance of purification, we can now turn to the next stage: fortification.

Fortification is strengthening the baseline systems, essentially building on top of the foundation that you have purified.

Breathing, drinking and eating are things we all do. But we rarely think about how much we need to do each. We can go 7 minutes without breathing, 7 days without drinking and 77 days without food.

Let's apply this ratio further. 7 minutes to 7 days is a ratio of 1-1440 (when considering the minutes in each), and that simply regards the ratio between breathing and drinking. So, if you need to make positive changes to your health, and you want to apply and fortify these changes into your lifestyle, then we need to work on what will have the biggest effects first. And what is easiest to change? Breathing, of course. In the purification segment above, I discussed the toxins in the air and how it is important to have clean air. Therefore, we now need to understand the importance of fortifying breathing, to ensure that you are consistently getting the right amount of quality air into your body.

While breathing might be the easiest thing to change, it is also the most important, the very reason I have chosen to focus on it first, in relation to fortification. It is not wise to jump straight to eating well, when the foundation it is based on relies intrinsically on first fortifying breathing and eating. Therefore, it is of the utmost importance that we first learn how to breathe properly.

You may be wondering why, but do you recall how I said that you have to create a good internal environment for your cells? Do you also remember that I discussed how adding something to your health routine won't help if you have a bad internal environment? Well, the same applies here. You will not get the same results if you work first on fortifying eating, for we have to build up from the basics. This is because breathing is the most important thing you can do.

Again, you can only last 7 minutes without air. So, surely, we want to make sure we get that right first? You need to change your state and breathing makes the biggest impact. If you went and changed your diet while not breathing properly or not being hydrated, you'd fail, crash and not get the results you desire. You would simply be rushing to the end of a process that requires a slow, steady and sustainable approach.

Understandably, you may well be thinking that you breathe all the time, so how can you do it better? Well, we often do not realise how we breathe shallowly, and fail to take advantage of the air reserves in our lungs. Optimal breathing requires optimal air, for one thing.

First, I want you to simply pay attention to your breathing. Where is your breath coming in from? Your chest, most likely.

Yet this is not optimal. To master optimal breathing, you should focus on your abdomen, *not* your chest.

So, how to breathe better?

Let's do an exercise.

Breathe in as deeply as you can, and into your belly. Keep your hand on your belly and let it fill out with air. Breathe in and out as fully as you can.

This is proper breathing. It will allow you to get the most amounts of oxygen in your body. This full breathing is the foundation of good health fortification. To start with, just practise this exercise once a day for a couple of minutes. This could be when you wake up, after you brush your teeth or simply whenever you get the time. Then start building up to what is comfortable for you. Perhaps do it for five minutes one day, then a bit more the next and so on, while making sure you do this *every day*.

How long and how often? Only you can assess this, and it will vary for each person. You will begin to identify the optimal amount of deep breathing for you when you notice the positive effects. I cannot tell you, just as I cannot tell you what food is good for you!

Only once you master this deep breathing and incorporate it daily, should you think about drinking properly.

Fortifying Your Water

While drinking well involves being hydrated, fortifying is about ensuring *constant* hydration. In the purifying stage, I emphasised the importance of clean water, filtered or mineral, and getting away from drinks with additives. Now, we need to work on maintaining proper hydration as a consistent part of our life.

Being dehydrated, while following all the other advice that both I give you and you learn from yourself, is like recycling dirty water to clean a house. Hydration refills your supply and allows you to better clean your body, your mind and your spirit. One act of drinking lots of water, whether just in the morning, over the course of a whole hour or lots throughout any given week, won't help long-term if you then return to being dehydrated.

Most people carry out their daily lives dehydrated, which is in part due to habit. People don't drink water because of the pace of life. It becomes an inconvenience to have water on hand and to regularly go to the bathroom. So, many people have developed a habit of not drinking enough water or drinking things that do not sufficiently hydrate them.

The thing is, the body is amazing, and it can function even if you're not fully hydrated. But this is *not sustainable*. The problem is that we tend to normalise being dehydrated, which, if this occurs too frequently, can lead your body to stop giving you signals to hydrate. If you feel thirsty, and you do not quench this thirst, your body will repeat the signal, before eventually giving up. This may lead you to not consistently staying dehydrated because you are no longer getting all the proper signals, which can lead to long-term health problems.

To remedy this, you have to get back in touch with your body to respond to its hydration needs. This notion, the need to attend to the messages our bodies give us, can be applied to any signal and cycle of the body. The sleep pattern, hunger, going to the toilet, whatever; they can all be ignored and repressed. We will come to that later on in more detail, but for now just try to pay attention to when you feel thirsty.

To combat this, you need to drink water consistently. You cannot simply drink a whole day's worth of water in the morning. This would be like eating your whole weeks' worth of meals on Monday — of course your body could not process all of this. So, you need to drink water and pay attention to how much you lose. As a side note, remember that if you spend time in air conditioning, you will lose more water as the air conditioning also dries out the air.

You may ask, can we not drink tea, coffee, or even green tea instead of water? Well, unfortunately, these things dehydrate you. Or they have additives in them that the body must use energy to exert. Now, I do not suggest you stop drinking tea and coffee (if you already currently do) at this very moment. You can instead simply incorporate them into the hourglass model. The main thing is to consistently drink water through the day to stay hydrated.

However, it is not enough to simply drink water. Many people don't realise that room temperature or hot water is better than cold. When you drink cold water from the refrigerator, an energy exchange takes place in your body to warm it up to then use it. Hot and room temperature water, on the other hand, saves your body's energy and can be used more efficiently. Think about it yourself: when you heat water in a kettle, you need energy, just as if you want to cool water in the fridge. The same is true for your body.

So, you need to drink water all day, ideally at room temperature or hot, for this is the best way to stay hydrated. Start by incorporating water as much as possible into your day, while avoiding other drinks. When you get this far, you will already be creating a considerably better health environment for yourself.

Both breathing and drinking are crucial for survival and good health. Remember the ratio of how long you can go without breathing, drinking and eating. You can go the longest without eating, a notion demonstrating how important and how effective good breathing and proper hydration are for your health. However, this does not mean we should stop there!

Fortifying Your Food

After you are able to fortify your breathing and drinking, it is time to move on to eating. I previously established the importance of the hourglass model for understanding *what* to eat. Yet to fortify, you should *consistently* be eating good quality food.

A lot of health books will simply try to explain what you should or shouldn't eat, while offering tricks and complicated diets. I take a different approach, aimed towards getting you to think about *what* you should eat, understand *how* food affects your body and implement this *sustainably*. This is why I gave you the hourglass model in the previous section, in order to help you work out *what* is good for you. However, in order to avoid putting the toxins back, you need to work on fortifying your health to enable sustainable and long-term dietary action, for which there are some crucial things to bear in mind.

The foundation of good eating is mainly that the food you eat should come from nature. In this respect, what you select should be very simple. When you go shopping, simply ask yourself, does it come from nature? Does it come from the ground, or is it taken from the sea or land? Is it made in a lab, packaged and artificial, or is it in fact something natural? With these thought processes, along with the knowledge you gain by implementing the hourglass model, you can very quickly find out what you should be putting into your body. This will allow you to create a good diet that works for you, that you both enjoy and want to stick to, because you will have based it on your internal recognition of what is good for *you*.

This mindset is very useful when you are shopping, for example when you ask yourself things like, "Can I drink coffee?" or, "Can I have pasta?" Think about where the items you buy come from, what is in them and what will be good for you, so you can develop a clear and efficient system that can help you make your decision.

Reinforcing the good food in your diet will allow you to maintain a positive level of health and eat the food that reacts well with you. By making sure it is not packaged or artificial, but rather made up of fresh ingredients you can find in nature, you will fortify your health, and increase nutrition. Additionally, because you will have fewer toxins in your body, you will have more energy for other things!

For understanding good food on a deeper level, think about the acronym **BENI**:

B stands for ***bioactive***, non-nutritive compounds. This is perhaps a bit of a mouthful, but simply encompasses everything that is not directly a vitamin or mineral, such as fibres, phytonutrients and special antioxidants that are present within food items.

E stands for ***energy***, and caloric content. This is basically how much chemical power can the body draw out of the food. For example, a piece of bread has around 70 calories worth of energy. At a modest 3.5 mph -- that's a pace of 17 minutes per mile -- a 125-pound individual burns 70 calories in about 17 minutes, 30 seconds.

N represents ***nutrients***, vitamins and minerals. This is where we get the bulk of nutrients which replenish our body's chemical stores. Your vitamins A to Zinc :)

I represents ***information***, about the food line. When it comes to information in food, science is finally catching up to say, "Hey, plants remember things from the chemical environment they're grown in, and it affects the kind of DNA expression that they have, or RNA expression that they have inside the actual plants."

Utilising good food, and good eating, relies upon an understanding of natural food, those with nutrients that benefit us. Plants growing in a natural environment will be much better than those interfered with or sprayed with chemicals. This is both obvious and intuitive.

So, effectively, think about what is in the food you are eating. Is it nutritious, how much energy will it give you and what is in it? Next time you are shopping, just pause and think about all of this for a moment.

At the same time, there is more to all of this than simply thinking about food differently; there are also implications for how you will see the world. Think about how you need to ensure your customers have a good experience, which is crucial for your company. For your success, you have to think about how the customers' experience relates to their goals, to then achieve your own goals of selling a product or service to them. From the bottom to the top of the company, the ecosystem is connected.

This is just the same with food and the planet. All of us can make a difference in any ecosystem if we have the interest to maintain it at every level. What is important here is that by making these internal introspections, and improving our health on an internal basis, we actually can make a positive difference in the external world.

When you think about the environment you want your food to be from, you will start to think about the world differently. You will build a new appreciation of how your food is created, who grows your food, how they feel and whether they are healthy. You will build an interest in ensuring the world is clean, and that there is really good, nutritional and natural food available both to you and others. We need to avoid toxins, yet how do we get fewer of them in our food and drink? We need less pollution. It is quite simple really. Without such an understanding, you cannot be healthy, nor succeed.

Amplifying

Finally, we move on to amplifying. After the stages of purifying the body and fortifying good behaviours, you now need to put these into a framework that will become a part of you. The first stage towards good health purifies your body and gets you to a baseline. The second stage helps begin to fortify good health, making it a part of you. The final stage, 'amplifying', embeds and enhances both elements within your life, so you can constantly and sustainably pursue the journey of good health. And crucially, it consists of three fundamental steps:

- **R**ituals
- **R**hythm
- **R**outine

In this context, the term amplifying means that we take good health and amplify it throughout ourselves at every level: the body, the mind and the spirit. In order to amplify, we must utilise the concept of seasonality, or rather the cycles of life. Our planet is built on cycles, and it is hard to conceptualise any portion of life that doesn't have cycles, from its larger absolutes to the microscopic. Indeed, the smallest things in our bodies divide, become tissue and then carry out their function. As well as this, we can look up to the cosmos, where there are cycles of stars that start as gas, condense into a solid object, before they finish burning their fuel and eventually explode or become a black hole. Everything, from the smallest to the biggest level, goes through cycles.

Essentially, amplification is the process of taking these small things that form the cycles within us, such as breathing, drinking and eating, that we do all the time, and scaling them up, making them part of us on a larger scale. While in one sense this helps our cells to be more efficient, which is the foundation, it all adds up to help us on the macro level. This then allows every part of us to synchronise and become a more authentic version of ourselves, where everything we do is what we want to, both consciously and subconsciously.

In general, a key aspect of amplification is repetition, to build momentum. Just as a rocket uses 90% of its fuel to get off the ground, you must build momentum from the foundational knowledge you acquire from this book (which is not whole without the wisdom you learn from yourself). This knowledge, too, can lift you up. Yet momentum can only be harnessed through implementation of these strategies on a consistent basis. When you repeat enough, each thing you do for good health will become second nature. Fundamentally, it is necessary to understand what your current habits are. And when it comes to thinking about the different health habits that a person has, we first need to analyse. In order to do this, we need to see things as they truly are. This requires brutal honesty, where we have to be truthful to ourselves so we can see where we are at. Once we have done that, we can then think about the future, and envisage it in a positive way. When you can envisage this brighter future, you can first set goals, before ultimately materialising them.

At the end of this section, you will have an exercise to help you with this. But first, you need to honestly reflect on what you do every day, every week and every month. This is not a matter of judgement, yet to make effective changes you need to understand exactly what you do regularly, without thinking. This will allow you to be in a position where you can work out what your good habits are, and what could do with being changed.

A lot of people get caught going backwards, because they tend to overthink the stage where they must contemplate the impact of their habits. This is where people start to read different things on the internet and listen to alternating opinions, confusing them as to what to do. For example, people might start to wonder things like, "Is eating this food every day actually bad for me? What about this exercise I like to do?" It is very easy to get conflicting information, because so much of it is out there. However, there is a strong guiding principle regarding how to analyse that information, which I want to emphasise. You do not have to accept it wholesale, but it can help you understand what you need to work on, all the while providing a handy conceptual tool to use!

This principle is that we are formed by energy — just as the universe was — and made of cells. These very cells themselves are ultimately energy, as well, which means that we can direct them. How we direct our energy is what is going to make this process flow forwards, facilitating an easy downhill slide. Or, if your energies are focused in the wrong direction, this will make it an uphill slog. How we focus on that and how we create that level of energy then helps us move in the direction that we want. Effectively, with a key goal to aim towards, while ultimately placing trust in yourself, this will be easier, and you won't get distracted by external information.

There is also another useful way to think about habits. For ultimately, humans are complex, and have lots of different driving factors, so it is helpful to consider these different ideas. Remember back to the different needs I outlined earlier:

- Certainty
- Significance
- Connection
- Love
- Growth
- Contribution

Meeting at least three of these needs from activities will make you, subconsciously, want to form a habit of that activity. When you do something where you get to connect with others, feel it is good for your health or gives you some significance, it is easier to make it a habit.

Also, there may be reasons based on these needs that you *don't* like certain activities. Perhaps you are shy because social activities make you feel uncertain or unloved. Yet, on the other hand, some people may love social interactions, because they feel a connection. The trick here is to identify how you feel when you do your habits. For example, if you do a physical activity with others and get a sense of connection from it, that will fit better into your lifestyle than an activity that didn't.

Therefore, identifying what you do now, and finding activities that can help you satisfy your needs, is an effective way to achieve sustainable health. When you note down your various habits, you can then reflect on what needs they fulfil. This will then equip you to better judge what habits are good, the ones that need changing and those that serve no purpose.

In one sense, even habits that are bad for our health can be good for our needs. For example, spending time at the pub may be bad for your physical health, but it can be good for your social needs. In these cases, you need to modify the behaviour that's bad for your physical health, while maintaining your needs. Using these needs will better equip. Using these needs will better equip you to sustainably implement positive habits into your lifestyle.

Above, we have touched upon how to analyse your habits, which will now allow us to work on the three steps of amplification: rituals, rhythms and routines. Each of these will help you incorporate good practices into a cycle that you can maintain, to remain healthy in a sustainable way. Rather than forcing a random diet or exercise regime into your lifestyle for a short period, I will instead focus upon the long-term adoption of good behaviours. And for this to be most successful, such an adoption must be carried out in a way that becomes second nature, *not* a chore.

Rituals - The Steady Platform

Rituals are things we do so often that we do not even think about them. You may think your morning ritual is something like 'wake up, brush my teeth, have a coffee', yet this passage skips so many small steps that are just as much of a ritual in your daily life. Take a moment to think about everything, big or small, that you do from the moment you wake up.

In actuality, when you wake up, you will get up a certain way. Perhaps you roll first, sit straight up, or carry out any other of the infinite ways to get out of bed, each of which is connected to how you prefer to sleep. Once you consider this, and every other little nuance, your morning ritual now becomes more like 'wake up on my left side, roll over, take a sip of water, stand on my left leg first, then my right, and walk to the bathroom'. These kinds of actions are done every day, and we do not think about them. Yet they are rituals, and indeed it is very important to think about what triggers your rituals.

For example, what precedes brushing your teeth on an average day? If you think back, you will realise that there are a range of small acts that come before this, each of which are just as much a part of your day. Personally, my typical morning involves waking up at 5 am, getting out of the left side of my bed and walking to the bathroom. But what if I were to wake up at 6? Well, maybe I would instead drink water first, or brush my teeth.

Now, it is not intentional that, when I wake up at different times, this influences my morning. Yet the change to my schedule can affect how I unconsciously engage with the world around me. Almost all of these rituals are completely unconscious; you don't even think about them. And this should act as strong motivation, because good health practices can also become unconscious parts of your day. You won't even think about them!

There are two layers of rituals, those that do not rely on the environment, and those that do. The first layer is those that are more stable, based on something more internal, and they do not change. The second layer, on the other hand, includes those that can be interrupted. For example, a phone call can interrupt your daily ritual of spending time with your children, or your work rituals.

What we have to do, then, is understand the trigger of these rituals. Why do we do them? We each have breathing, drinking and eating rituals. And these may be a part of the reason your health isn't where you know it should be. Understanding this, and building an awareness of our unhealthy rituals, then allows us to begin to change them.

As many rituals depend on triggers, we can change the trigger. It is much easier to adapt those rituals that depend on something else, by changing what it is they depend on. You can interrupt your morning routine to include some deep breathing, for example, when you work out the trigger for your standard breathing. If you typically eat or drink something in the morning, work out what precedes this, interrupt it and incorporate water and some healthier food.

A good ritual can include things such as ensuring you start the day breathing properly. Or drinking water first thing to ensure that you immediately begin to hydrate yourself after you wake up. Other options could be doing a small physical activity to keep yourself active, including healthy food in your meals, or meditating and reflecting on your emotions.

Evidently, there are all sorts of things that a good ritual can include. Yet the point is, in order to amplify your good health practices, you must make them a ritualistic part of your day, to the point where you no longer think about them.

The first step is to identify your current rituals, to work towards changing them for the better. If you are able to identify the initial trigger of your rituals, you can then hook on any other beneficial ritual that you want to develop into your life. For example, if you wanted to develop a pattern of breathing, and currently don't really breathe from your belly but rather from your chest, there are a whole bunch of different ways to develop the habit. But one of the strongest ways to actually help anchor it into your daily life is to hook it onto something that you already do automatically.

Say if you brush your teeth at the exact time every day, no matter how stressed you get, how much sleep you get, or what is going on in your life, then that would be a good place to anchor breathing exercises onto this ritual. These might then become a natural part of your morning, and the next thing you know you could be doing proper breathing without thinking. This also applies to any other good practice.

To anchor something you should think, "Okay, what do I do that initiates that particular action, and what thought patterns are coming during this time when I brush my teeth?" You should work out the sensation inside your body that leads to that action. Once you know that feeling, you can reroute it to then say, "When I feel this, I am going to first take a deep abdominal breath, and then brush my teeth." By simply sending out that little connection, what will happen is that even if you miss it, you will be brushing your teeth, and then suddenly go, "Oh, right, I was supposed to actually take a deep breath!" So, the trigger, because it is so far ahead, will go back and then reinforce it, even though you might have forgotten it to start off with.

By attaching new actions to current rituals, you can create a chain of associations that are easier to follow and adapt into. As I mentioned, the first step is to be aware of your current rituals. Create a document, excel table, or whatever works for you, and try to make notes on what fills your time, every day. Try to get as granular as possible, but if you prefer the big picture to start with, that is okay — you can break down the smaller steps later on the more you think. But if you can identify the different things you do with your time, and the chain of events, you will be able to think about where to begin to make positive changes. For now, however, don't stress too much about making these changes, just identify what you currently do.

Rhythms - The Cycles on Top of the Platform

In this context, rhythm refers to your body's *daily* rhythm, which is like an orchestra. In an orchestra, you have each specific section, such as the strings, the brass and the woodwind, each doing their own sound. When their rhythm is in sync, you get a beautiful symphony. Yet when the rhythm is out of sync, merely a bad sound.

Our bodies similarly have different rhythms that are interconnected, which can synchronise, leading to a harmonious lifestyle, where everything you do is directed to what you want. This occurs when your higher goals are actualised, and your mind, body and spirit work together. Or, your rhythm can struggle to be synchronised, which leads to friction.

Take your sleep rhythm, something all of us have, which can frequently vary. My patients often say to me, "I can't get up early in the morning and be productive." When this comes up, I reply, "Great, don't force it, learn your rhythm." But this goes deeper than mere sleep. Some times of the day are for being creative, and others to be focused. You need to understand this rhythm, basing your day and your life around it. For example, if you know that you are most creative at 10 am, this is not the time to be doing work on a repetitive task. If you synchronise your different rhythms, you will get better results. You just have to feel your body, feel your mind, and learn how to synchronise them.

If you force yourself to work at a time when you are not productive, your body's rhythm will become out of sync, which could have a knock-on effect towards other areas of your bodily rhythms. In addition, you might eat at a time your body isn't hungry or socialise when you need time to yourself. I don't know what exactly, but in each of these cases you would not be acting in accordance with yourself, nor towards your goals. You would instead be working with a bad rhythm, out of sync, leading you to being less productive, less happy and generally unable to achieve your goals.

Therefore, we have to work on identifying when you feel hungry or thirsty, when you have the best energy for physical activity, when you are most productive for work, when you should sleep and so on. This will allow you to fit everything else in your life: your rituals, your habits and fulfilling your needs, in an optimal manner for you. This requires you to pay attention to your behaviours, your moods and any signals your body gives you.

With this understanding, we can now get into amplification in more detail, by talking about routines.

Amplifying Routines

With an understanding of your ideal rituals and rhythms, you can then make a routine that maintains the positive rituals in unison with the rhythms that work best for you. This is something similar to inversion, because it is like life planning, but in reverse. Most people say, "I'm going to do *this, this and this,* and then I'll deal with the consequences." "I'm going to get up early, go for a jog, do my chores, and then do all my work before 3 pm," for example. But this is backward.

Think instead of what you know about your body and your rhythms. Question yourself: how does my body function? How does my brain function? How do these rhythms that I know work with this plan? Contemplating each of these will allow you to work out your routine based on the facts you already know about yourself. If you know when you are most creative, most productive and most awake, build your routine around that. This, in conjunction with all the previous steps, will amplify and consolidate the good behaviours, and improve your health. In turn, this will allow you to direct your spirit wherever you want to go.

What you will have noticed is that the basis of this is awareness. Be aware of your current rituals, rhythms and routines. Then we can make the changes, bit by bit. You can then ensure that, instead of your usual breakfast, you have a healthier one. Instead of that sugary coffee, you have water. You can work out what kinds of work are best done at certain times. This way you will get better results. Not just from your health, by knowing when and what to eat or when and what to do for exercise, but because you will be a more productive person. This will facilitate a harmonisation of all the different moving parts that make you a person, allowing you to plan your day to get the most out of it, and therefore get the most out of your life!

Health Vision

One absolute need for good health is a *health vision*. This can tie into the previously discussed spiritual component of health, as it is about a large-scale vision that can be part of your self-actualisation. It can be something to help us connect with ourselves on a deeper level. This health vision will guide you towards good health, acting as an example to hold yourself to, to aim toward and to direct your cells towards achieving.

Ask yourself this: how do you imagine your health to be in a year, or five, ten and so on? Do you have a specific goal to achieve? How are you taking the steps to get there? What do you think you need to do? For example, if you feel you need to have more energy, or lose more weight, in order to take part in an endurance sporting event, such as a triathlon, let this vision guide you in your decisions. Track your activities, water intake, diet and exercise, all of which will help you aim toward your health vision. At the end of this book, when you better understand your psychological blocks, thus enabling you to break your inner demons, you will be able to create your own plan and track yourself accordingly.

Perhaps you can think about it this way. If I gave you a timeline and said, "In 12 months, you are going to be in the best health that you could have ever imagined," you might say to me, "I have no idea what that will look like." So, pick a time in your life when you did have good health. However you think about it, try to make an image of what you understand good health to be, based on your own understanding of yourself.

This also factors into spiritual and mental health, too. You should think: what is good mental and spiritual health? How can I move towards that as much as possible? Regardless of your faith, or lack thereof, or even your current mental well-being, you will have some inner understanding of what is or isn't good health. You can then use this as something to aim towards.

Having a health vision, and telling yourself you can achieve it, is a key way to achieve success in your health quest. There was once a study called 'The Power of the Pygmalion Effect: Teachers' Expectations Strongly Predict College Completion', involving a group of teachers with three different groups of children, which demonstrates this well. The teachers were told that there were three groups: one that was the highest level of intellect and would achieve the best scores, but also misbehaved; a middle group with a mix of abilities; a third group with learning and behavioural difficulties, whose goal was to learn just a 10th of the curriculum. Unsurprisingly, the children's results reflected what the teachers were told.

However, they repeated the study, where they put the worst kids in the first group, telling the teachers that they would in fact be the best students, yet they get bored easily and so sometimes misbehaved. In this scenario, it was this group that achieved the best scores. The middle group stayed the same, but the best students, put in the worst group, actually did worse!

The expectations of the teachers affected the student's outcomes. It works for you as well. If you expect failure, you will fail, yet if you expect success, you can achieve it. If you have a health vision and believe it is real, you can reach that level of good health!

Summary of Good Health

I will now summarise what was discussed throughout this chapter, before offering more easily implementable action items to engage with! You, as a successful person, have most likely sacrificed health in your pursuit. Yet if you do not make a change, then you will suffer, and potentially die earlier. It is important to understand, however, that you can alter this.

And how do we have good health?

Well, I do not focus on the *external*, but instead the *internal*. Cells make tissue, which makes organs, which make systems. So, making healthy cells naturally then makes a healthy human. And this in turn links to the human mind, and how we think.

We should ultimately consider ourselves as made of energy. The universe is made of energy, as indeed we are at the cellular level. We can, therefore, direct our energy in different directions, ones that can lead to positive results.

Similarly, you need a health vision that you can direct yourself towards achieving.

While breathing, drinking and eating well are external, engaging with each in a beneficial way ultimately comes down to tapping into an inner knowledge of what is good for you, and what your body wants, so you can make the correct decisions. Utilising the information imparted throughout this chapter will allow you to do so, as you begin to find the answers within you. Right now, you are likely distracted. Distracted by the things you have been told about good health. Distracted by your work. Distracted by whatever. But still, your body is screaming for you to do something. This is why you are reading this book, because somewhere inside you, you know that you are not as healthy as you should be. What this book has offered up to this point, and will continue to do so, is to get you in tune with who you are inside, find your baseline and make what is within you identifiable.

To be healthy, we begin with purifying ourselves, at every level, by working on our breathing, drinking and nutrition, to improve the health of our cells. Then we listen to our bodies and learn our rituals and routines, improve them, and eventually synchronise everything to make it all a part of us. What this requires, in the ultimate mission for good health, is looking into yourself. For without this insight, we cannot direct our spirit in the *way* we want, nor attain *what* we want.

Most likely, as an entrepreneur, you have previously failed to take into account everything I just told you, because you were too busy trying to change the world. Yet now is the time to change yourself. By starting this journey by looking inward, you will be better equipped to make the impact on the world that you want to. I want you to turn inwards, find the answers inside yourself, and shape your reality from the inside out. Rather than just trying to affect the external world, realise the importance of the internal. For this is the fundamental philosophy at play here. Your body is amazing. My body is amazing. All of our bodies are amazing. Each of our bodies work hard on detoxifying and looking after all of us. However, we all have a weak link. If your body is full of toxic things, such as mercury from eating too much fish, and if your joints happen to be your weakest link, then you will develop joint pain secondary to the mercury toxicity. Or perhaps you are regularly breathing bad air, because of pollution nearby. Maybe you drink water full of toxins. Even if you are generally consuming what you believe is natural, if you are not working with both your breathing and hydration, then you will struggle to improve your health.

Simultaneously, if after reading this chapter you feel that the advised strategies are too much to deal with, remember that this is an *understandable* apprehension. Yet I assure you that applying them will be easier than it sounds, as long as you do each component one at a time. We will slowly reduce the bad things in your lifestyle, and one by one, improve.

You should now have a broad idea of some of the steps to take to learn from *yourself,* in order to be healthier. This can be achieved by learning what works for you, through thinking about what you already know, internally, surrounding what makes you healthier. You already know drinking water is good, and that things which grow in good conditions will be better for you. You may not realise it, but you also know when the best times to sleep, work and be creative are. So now, the task is simply to bring out more of this information from yourself, using the tools imparted throughout this chapter, and apply it, all in the knowledge that a brighter future can be reached.

To conclude, turn the next page for further steps you can put in place today, to continue your health journey.

Action Items 3

To start with, create a document or table where you can track your daily activities. This will include breathing, drinking, eating and feelings in columns, and a date/time slot column as well. How you do this is up to you, but whatever format selected should allow you to be able to track all these activities.

1. **Pay attention to your breathing and try to breathe deeply every day.**

Remember to breathe in fully, into your belly, and breathe out fully as well. Track how often you do this, and for how long, and make notes of it every day. For example:

- "On Monday, I did proper breathing for 5 minutes."
- "On Tuesday, I extended this to 10 minutes."

And so on…

2. **Start to hydrate with room temperature or hot water.**

Drink water as much as possible, until you have clear urine. And similarly to proper breathing, keep track of the quantity you drink every day. How many litres did you drink? Did you drink anything else? Write it down!

3. **Pay attention to what you eat, and how it reacts with your body.**

Track three things regarding your diet: what you eat, how you feel physically after eating these foods and your mood, while also note any other effects that happen after eating. In your notes, try to write as it happens, rather than too long a time after, and draw out any correlations. For example:

- "Ate fresh fruit at 12 pm."
- "Felt energised at 12.30 pm."

4. **Listen to your body's rhythm and make notes, so you can adjust your habits accordingly.**

Feel sleepy at 3 pm? Creative at 7 pm? Are you hungry at certain times? Listen to your body, and begin to adjust your schedule, in order to work out your rhythm!

5. **After becoming familiar with your rhythm, and trying to breathe and hydrate, you can then consider trying to remove just *one* thing from your diet, and see how you feel.**

To help with this, continue to monitor your feelings and see if you can relate your food intake to them. Write out any correlations, good or bad. For the bad ones, try to remove them from your diet, while including more of those that seem to induce a positive reaction.

If you notice your health feels better when you cut out red meat, continue to live without it. If you notice that cutting white meat made no change, or made you worse, then you know it in fact reacts well with your body and should be retained. However, remember to only cut out one thing at a time, so that the effect it has on your body becomes clear.

6. **Begin to make positive changes a habit, starting with small measures.**

For example, practise your breathing, include water in your daily routine and take a small walk at the same time every day, in order to build consistency of these actions so that they can be sustainably implemented long-term. Make notes of what you do, and how this makes your body feel. Incorporate just one action at a time, and remember to focus on breathing, then water, then food before, ultimately, more mindful and spiritual exercises.

7. **Do things that are achievable now, in accordance with your body and mind's routine.**

You do not need to do everything right now. Do not simply abandon all food apart from fruit and veg, while taking up an hour of daily running at this exact moment. You will not be able to sustain this. Instead, simply ensure that you start, steadily adding incremental steps and actions as you build up to a daily routine that works for both you and your health.

Part 2

Working With Your Subconscious

By fundamentally dealing with how to understand yourself, this section of the book will explain the underlying reasons in our minds that make us struggle to achieve our health goals, and how to deal with them. You will learn about what is within you, how you can modify your subconscious behaviours and how to learn from inside yourself. All of this will encompass an exploration of your mind and spirit, with a strong emphasis on your intuitive intelligence and subconscious.

When you get to the end, you will see yourself in a new way, and be better able to synchronise all aspects of yourself.

This may appear to you as a bit irrelevant to your health, but your mind is as much a part of you as your body. Your subconscious is what drives many of your actions, while your body often sends you signals that you have lost sight of the very things that can help you make the right decisions for better health. All of this, and more, is what we are about to dive into. So, let's go!

Chapter 4

Are You Wired for Bad Health?

To begin, this chapter will explore the importance of acknowledging that each of our minds have been hijacked, but that *now* is the time to change this programming.

Are you wired for bad health? That's what often comes to mind as a question for many people, the answer to which is usually, "Oh, I don't know, maybe I am."

People often think they cannot change, overcome their cravings or do anything differently. They think that no matter what they do, or what diets they practise, they will always gain weight. That they can never resist gorging on bad foods, or that exercise is quite simply something that they could never incorporate into their daily lives. They are hard-wired, as far as they think, to be unhealthy. This chapter will work through this idea, that I have come to learn many people have — a sense of hopelessness, the idea you cannot change and that health is just too difficult.

As an entrepreneur, you may resent the idea of something being hard, instead preferring to relish in the challenge, or perhaps you feel strapped for the time necessary to invest in your health. Or, you may think, "Well, sure, I should be healthier, but that's not what I have ever succeeded in, so I can't start now!"

This is a lie; you can do it.
Anyone can have good health.

Do you think there are certain junk foods you just cannot live without? Or that you will never be able to feel happy and calm? Do you think that no matter what you try, you will always fail? Perhaps you think a healthy lifestyle just 'isn't for you'?

The problem is that your intuitive health compass has been hijacked, both from a physical and a mental/emotional point of view. You may think that your behaviours are unchangeable because you cannot conceive of thinking any differently, having become so used to doing so in a certain way.

However, you must come to understand that there are certain things, of which you may not even realise, that are holding you back from good health. This is due to your mind being hijacked, both by the lies passed down to you by your parents and peers. But everything *can* be changed, and you *can* have good health, as well as being able to stick with it in a sustainable way!

The Bliss Point

On a nutritional level, you have most likely become addicted to wanting what can be described as the 'bliss point', a concept that scientists in the food industry have discovered and increasingly utilised. Let me explain.

What this term means is that you receive happiness, a short rush and a sense of bliss, from various food items that are bad for you. The combination of salt, sugar and fat contained within a lot of these processed items that I label as "non-foods", gives you that optimum and immediate endorphin hit. Then the endorphins from these foods turn these non-food items into things that you crave.

This effectively makes us become dependent on this rush. The food scientists know where this bliss point is, and thus ensure their product has this effect. For example, Domino's pizza has sugar in both its sauce and dough. This isn't by mistake, for it allows those eating the product to experience this 'bliss point', which can effectively become addictive, while warping our relationship with food on a physical level.

This is very similar to how many people depend on caffeine in the mornings, even though you can have plenty of energy, which people seek from the beverage, if you simply eat well. You don't actually need coffee for energy. Caffeine creates a dependency and addiction that causes a vicious cycle, where if you cut it out you may feel low initially, but eventually you can be a more efficiently functioning person. In fact, you can most likely be more energetic without it!

On the topic of sugar, while it used to simply be a luxury, it has now been added to so many parts of our everyday diets, while often being associated with celebrations such as Halloween or Christmas. It is in so many foods, and because of how our body processes different sugars, a slice of white bread can actually spike you more than pure sugar, in terms of energy! These energy spikes you get from sugar can lead to overcorrecting, which in turn can lead to you crashing. This stimulates appetite, because your body is trying to smooth out this imbalance. Therefore, you can end up eating more as a direct result of eating things with lots of sugar.

Having all this sugar can have many negative effects. It can affect your risk of heart disease, diabetes, weight gain and give you bad skin problems. Furthermore, overuse of sugar can damage the mouth, teeth and gums, while also potentially leading to autoimmune problems through inflammation in lots of parts of the body.

You may think, "Okay, so I should replace sugar with artificial sweetener, then," but the exact same reactions take place in the body when you ingest these sweeteners. The body responds, so you get hungry and eat more. But what makes this even worse than having sugar is you don't get the highs, so the people who follow these diets end up feeling down. This all illustrates how our treatment of a product which can be very bad for us has changed over time, from a luxury to a necessity. At the same time, marketing and social norms have normalised the mass eating of sugar. The thing is, overall, that your gut's health is linked to your *whole* health, so taking care of what you are ingesting is essential.

Marketing and Myths

Returning to the main point, we have on one side of the coin a physical dependence on the bliss point. On the other hand, from the mental/emotional point of view, some ideas have been given to us that have completely warped our understanding of health.

One main issue is how companies utilise marketing and advertising. They aim to insinuate ideas that are not remotely true about what is healthy and give you the illusion that their product is the most important thing to have. This includes things like the idea that breakfast is the most important meal of the day, or that you should drink milk for strong bones. These are all illusions, which can brainwash someone from a very young age. That's the problem. So many ideas we have about healthy or unhealthy eating have come not from actual research, but rather from marketing and advertising, and it is so insidious that we don’t even question them.

This is firstly a generational issue, because your parents didn't really know better. They were taught things from television, and from their own parents who were told incorrect information, and so on. I believe cold showers are good for health, but my parents would be deeply alarmed at this idea, as it is one that is not held within their own cultural understanding of health, which emphasises heat. Conversely, I don’t drink cold water, yet so many people think it is better for quenching thirst. Think of how advertisements use ice-cold-looking drinks. These are things that we have been told and learned from, but never really thought about.

Generally, then, you inherit a lot of these ideas, and believe them without question on a subconscious level, which underpins a lot of the struggle. Those are the main lies you start to inherit as children, as our parents start to repeat the things they see on TV and in advertisements. Therefore, we often approach food and drink all wrong, without knowing what we are really doing, nor why. We don't know why we struggle to make a change, and when no improvements are ultimately made, feel as though we are hardwired for bad health.

These lies, no matter where they are from, determine your daily routine. This affects what you put inside your body, which in turn affects your health. For example, perhaps you think you need to eat three meals a day and end up overeating when you are not hungry. Or you think you need to drink lots of milk, thus not properly hydrating yourself. Or you think that if you eat products that call themselves superfoods, you will lose weight, so you overeat them every day. It doesn't matter which you do, and I can imagine that most who read this may have fallen for at least one of these.

Don't take it personally, we have all made these mistakes. The people behind these misconceptions are very good at what they do. It's a whole industry, filled with people working out how to get you to buy their products. No matter how smart you may be, you are at a disadvantage when it comes to marketing. Marketing ideas are honed for months, going through multiple iterations to get certain responses. When you encounter some marketing, advertising or even the layout of a supermarket, it is all designed as a mind trap.

Even I, who am trained in neuroscience, can read something like a website and take its word without realising it is marketing. It has become extremely clever and advanced at this point. We as humans receive information from the world around us. It enters our subconscious even if we aren't aware of it. There is so much contradictory information out there that makes it hard to make good decisions. Both your nature and environment are intrinsically used against you.

In addition to marketing and ideas from your parents, social and communal peer pressure to eat a particular way very much exists, which can heavily influence your routine around food. This comes at a societal level from advertising, but also from how your parents or your friends treat food. We can often see people get excited about food on the basis of taste alone, ignoring the health effects attached to them. This leaves us, in turn, treating food the same way.

When you go on a diet, you feel you deny yourself something tasty, and this is the biggest issue, because taste is a priority for you. You see your friends eating food that is bad for them, but because everyone does it, you do too. You go to celebrate a holiday where everything is built around food. You feel that you are being rude or missing out on something if you don’t eat or drink like everyone else. This is heavy peer pressure!

Yet now is the time to fight back, and do what is right for *you*, even if no one else follows.

How to Approach Health

Social attitudes to food completely warp our relationships with it from what they ideally should be. To explain, there is a difference between someone who is eating for health versus eating for pleasure. When someone goes into a restaurant and chooses what to eat, peer pressure often makes us look at food only on the basis of pleasure. In other words, we are trained to eat for pleasure, and seek this pleasure in these "non-foods".

Due to this, we often do not look at food in the right way in the first place. Nor do we approach food as something for nutrition or health, but rather, again, just for our pleasure. For example, do you avoid certain foods just because you think they are not that tasty? When choosing between meals, what is the determining factor? Usually taste, right? Or cravings? Yet this is not the correct way to approach food. Now, I am not saying good food cannot taste good, but these notions are certainly a testament to how we currently value food in society.

In addition, perhaps you look at food merely as a necessity, without considering what you put inside yourself. If you eat three times a day because that's what you have always done, you have fallen victim to food myths. The method of fasting demonstrates this well, which millions of people do, whereby you realise how long you can go without food. Indeed, we don't need to eat as often as we think; we *only* need to eat when we're hungry. I will explore this idea further in a later chapter, but this is an example of how, rather than listening to ourselves as we should, we instead often rely on ideas that were given to us from external sources.

So, how most people approach food and health is all a combination of their brain's desire for endorphins, and the myths they learn from advertising, parents and others.

You may have noticed that so far I have almost entirely been talking about food, in spite of the fact that this chapter is about being wired for bad health, overall. Well, of course, other topics relate to this. However, food and nutrition, and drinking properly, are some of the clearest examples of how we have had our innate intuitive intelligence hijacked by misinformation from others. If you think you cannot make changes to your health, a lot of this mindset may be rooted in the ideas passed on to you, that you accept as unbreakable.

It is also necessary to talk about the importance of what we associate with good health. I explained previously that breathing, water and nutrition all go a long way to creating a healthy internal environment in your body. This relates to the issue of feeling wired for bad health. We often focus only on food or exercise, ignoring the importance of water and breathing. Even if you don't make a change in your physical activity, but do make the right steps towards improving your relationship with drinking water and eating good food, your health will improve immensely. It will certainly improve more than if you *just* exercised.

Approaching food and drink with the right attitude means to want to replenish your life force, as opposed to simply quenching your hunger. This is a big difference. We need to see food and drink not purely in relation to taste, but rather as giving you life force. At the same time, you have to stay hydrated with water, as it is the very hydration this enables that will sustain your health long-term. Crucially, hydration underpins and supports the various other components that also combine to support improved health. One of these is good, nutritious foods, that you should learn to desire over others, because this will above all else provide your body with what it needs.

Everything counts, either adding or subtracting, supporting or destroying. We often don't think that everything we do is important, but it all adds up. So when you give in to doing bad things too frequently, even if you think you generally live a healthy life, you will eventually sink slowly into bad health: "Oh, a little bit of this, a little bit of that, it doesn't really matter." A glass of sugary drink here, some artificial food there. It's just a little bit, right? And that's where it starts, leading to having all of the different toxicities inside our system, which build up from the small things we do. If these negative actions start to combine, then you will end up in bad health. By overloading yourself with even the smallest of these actions, the ship that is your body will sink because of all the leaks. So, you need to make changes.

However, the flip side is also true, whereby small things can also add up in a positive way. If you are thirsty, for example, have a glass of water, instead of reaching for juice or a fizzy drink. Or when you have a lot of energy, go for a walk, instead of sitting on the couch while streaming an endless supply of shows. These actions will add up and combine in ways that produce results you never thought possible. For, ultimately, only a small start is required as you embark upon this journey.

We often believe that we ought to automatically know what to do to both remove toxicities and have great health. After all, it's common sense, right? We all know that water is good for you, fruit and veg are things you should have in your diet, and that you shouldn't live a sedentary life. Yet many of us are not in good health. We are often dehydrated, eat food with a lot of things that are bad for us and put off the positive actions we ought to be applying ourselves towards. So, something is clearly not adding up.

Well, I have come to learn that, too often, common sense is not apparent among the general public as frequently as the name might suggest. Perhaps having the correct mindset should instead be called 'uncommon sense', as most people often act in accordance with a herd mentality that is not beneficial to their health. It is this very herd mentality that in fact makes *common* sense incredibly *uncommon*. When everybody runs down the street, we tend to simply turn around and join them, even though we do not know what we're running away from. If common knowledge was all that was needed, then surely everyone would have the results that we all want, right? However, so many people remain out of shape, unfit and unhealthy, yet are in the same environment as those who are not. Therefore, in order to attain uncommon sense, you have to surround yourself and begin to associate with the uncommon people, who share the necessary mindset conducive to both success and health.

To find these other people to look to, who will allow you to escape this sense of peer pressure, you may find yourself needing to change your habits for a while, as you start on your health journey. Perhaps your social interactions will change, or how you approach certain holidays. Yet this should all be focused as part of your attempt to stop seeking external validation, which is the most sustainable solution to developing the mindset necessary for long-term health improvements.

Now, all of this may seem a bit negative. I have been telling you all the ways that you have been lied to; how we approach food and drink wrong; the ways in which we lack common sense. So, are you wired for bad health?

No, you're *not*!

We can make changes. We can adapt our behaviours and train ourselves to view the world entirely differently. Understanding these influences is one of the most crucial steps, that will allow you to set yourself apart from and outpace those around you. Because the mistake most people make is to go through life without ever questioning why they eat the way they do. You now have the tools to do so.

How to 'Rewire'

After having established that each of us have been deceived regarding our health, we can now talk about how to change our mindset. For example, let's start with how to not be influenced by others so much. To shift out of herd mentality into *uncommon sense,* you have to become present with what is around you. For example, if you shop at the mall, which hosts endless unhealthy fast-food places, and you then get hungry, what happens?

Even if you generally eat good food, with the right mindset, in this environment your ability to sustain this goes down. Indeed, your good habits will go *down* as your hunger goes *up,* especially with the immediate choices available. All of a sudden, your usual dietary preferences fail, because surrounding you is nothing but junk food, while you are hungry and don't have the time to find an alternative, nor the willingness to wait until later. You go along with the herd, and the next thing you know you are eating some completely artificial junk food that offers zero nutritional value. Then you feel bad about it after. This is certainly a universal experience we have all encountered, at some point or another!

One of the ways to counter this is to look at the people in line for that particular food, and ask yourself, "Does this represent how I want to look? Does their energy level represent how I want to feel?" Instead of looking at the food, look at the people standing in front of each booth, and it may help your choice. You may be able to convince yourself to wait a while until you can access something genuinely good for you. Try to snap out of the herd mentality, in order to not get into that line and think merely about convenience.

Often people just say, "Oh, there's a line, so it must be good," and then join it. Yet presence stops that. Presence makes you aware of what you are doing, and if you really want to take part in something. Presence is an amazing tool through which to simply ask if the action you are about to do is what you want. Does it fit your goal, and are these people around you who you want to follow? Likely not.

Similarly, most people do not have common sense regarding how to deal with toxins, or how to be healthy. We generally just follow what others do and fall for the lies that are around us. The thing is, the true answers are not external, and they do not come from other sources. When you observe the general health of most people, why are you really listening to them anyway? When you think about how many companies are just trying to make money, why do we listen to their advertising ideas?

Because in fact, the real answers come from within ourselves. No one knows what is good for you like you do! You need to use your health vision to guide yourself, to pause and reflect whenever you are instinctively going to eat or do something that could affect your health. Ultimately, wouldn't you feel happier if you were healthier, than if you caved in and ate that junk food? Use this thought process to reflect on the actions you really want to take, and to change how to approach food— especially when it comes to peer pressure or situations where you feel your resolve is slipping.

In addition, you can employ inversion to consider what the best thing to do would be. Ask yourself, "I could either wait until I get home to eat the healthy food in my fridge or eat at this food stand in the mall. But which is worse for my health?" You will get your answer pretty quickly.

Effectively, all of this represents being aware of what you are doing, an awareness that is the start of making effective change It sounds simple, and in a way it is, but it is something that you have to practise.

Taking this moment to pause and reflect on what you *really* want, in the big picture, while delaying the gratification of short-term pleasure in exchange for your health goals, is a good skill to work on. It will give you the ability to guide yourself and stop being influenced by herd mentalities or the lies you have inherited. You can do it!

To finish, I want to share with you a story of a famous experiment, The Stanford Marshmallow Experiment. The research team got a group of children, brought them into a room, and offered them all a marshmallow. Yet they also said if they waited, they could have two in ten minutes. The kids who refused the first marshmallow and were willing to wait for the second were actually those who scored better in various metrics later in life, such as exams and health. Now, there are various factors here, but willpower does play into delayed gratification, and then a better lifestyle. If you can focus on the big picture, you will find success in other areas.

You are not wired for bad health. In the course I offer, each week we engage with different psychological components, to discover what is inside of an individual person. And one of the key principles we explore is that everything that you need is literally within you, as you will have already come to learn thus far. This focus is because it is so important to work on. The fact that you have had your intuitions hijacked, and that your mind is full of ideas that were passed down for you, means that such a mindset is not hardwired. It is all changeable. The trick, now, is to start inspecting yourself, and make changes to the things that you've never even thought about. Somewhere in your mind are the answers, as well as the ability, even subconsciously, to live a healthy life. Now is simply the time to find these, and apply them consistently.

Internal Over External Validation

As I have previously touched upon, one crucial psychological tool is to avoid looking to others for the answers, and that internal motivation is better than external. Have you ever had an experience whereby you felt great doing the right thing, without anyone congratulating you? It feels good right? You don't need validation to know you did the right thing.

Once we understand that we have everything we need inside of us, what are we looking outside for? Validation? Yet I again stress that you *don't* need validation from external sources. These external sources could be something such as a prescribed health target from a magazine, like losing a certain amount of weight or running a number of miles, or they could come from the approval of others. Perhaps it is because you want to be like certain people you know. However, none of this is really *sustainable*. Usually, you will fall back to old habits, because once you reach that goal, it won't last. Or the goal is not truly attainable, and when you do not reach it you feel as though you have failed, before giving up on health altogether. Either way, the need for this form of validation is not an effective long-term solution.

Instead, your motivation must be internal. You should not eat what others do simply because this is what they say — you should eat what aligns with what *you* know is good for you. You should not live your life on the basis of what others do, but instead completely remove any consideration of their behaviour, or attitudes, in whatever you do. Don't aim for good health because you want people to congratulate you, or to merely achieve a certain weight. You should want to do it because you know it is the right thing, and that good health is intrinsically beneficial.

As an entrepreneur, good health leads to greater success. You will be able to go a lot longer than if you continue the way you have been living so far. To do this, you must understand that only your own, self-prescribed and discovered health goals, health vision, and the answers within you, are what matter. Try to understand using this health vision as sixth-dimensional thinking, when envisaging your overall big picture vision. What this means is to look *beyond the present,* and *towards the future.*

Connect this image of who you want to be, of what this picture of good health is, and connect this within your five senses. Picture yourself in the future and what you will look like. Imagine yourself doing something that you know is good for your health. Imagine how things smell, taste, feel and so on, and attach this to what you saw in your sixth sense vision. Sixth sense vision is the vivid replaying of a future anticipated outcome in the mind.

By linking the here and now with the future, you can help to make your health vision a reality, as you discover actions that you can direct every part of your body towards.

Again, you are not wired for bad health. If you look around you, imagine the big picture of what you want to be, and try to align it with your actions. This will allow you to take a big step towards a change in yourself. The fact is that all of the problems I outlined earlier; the behaviours we have learned; the lies that we have accepted about food; the bad attitudes to food and drink; the peer pressure; the lack of common sense — we *learned* all of them. Yet that also means we can unlearn them. We *can* learn better behaviours, for we were not simply born with those we currently engage. With just a little work, each of these can be changed.

Ultimately, your body is incredible. Your skin is crawling with thousands of different bacteria. Yet if we remove too many of them, we lose our natural protection. When you are a toddler, and you begin to explore your environment, you eat different foods and already start to absorb toxic things from the environment. Yet despite all this, we can still actually be okay. We survive, we live, we grow up, and we have functioning lives. We come into contact with viruses and bacteria all the time. Yet most of the time we fight them off. It is only when our immune system is weak and we deal with something for the first time that we struggle, but our bodies react for a reason, in order to deal with the problem and get stronger.

We still need to detoxify, and make sure we live a healthy life, but the point is that your body is incredible. At the same time, if your body is balanced and you have strong inner health, you can withstand new bacteria and new viruses much better.

Therefore, you are not wired for bad health. In fact, your body is rather strong — you just need to give it better balance. When you begin to understand this, you can learn that the solution to your health issues comes from within, not externally.

That being said, there are of course actions you need to take to improve your health, as I discussed in the previous chapter. However, one of the reasons you may think you are wired for bad health is that you are daunted by the actions you need to do. These can appear overwhelming, impossible and too much. Well, in response to this, I want to discuss the 80/20 rule, in relation to the 1/50 rule. The 80/20 rule has many uses, while it is often said that "20% of actions create 80% of the results." If this is the case, 20% of the things you do everyday result in 80% of your health. But 20% can sometimes feel more than you can do.

Let's take this to the 3rd degree. What is the 80/20, of 80/20 of 80/20? The answer is 1/50. So, let's consider this; what is the 1% of actions that account for 50% of your results?

Ask yourself, "What is the 1% step in developing habits that will give me 50% of the results I want to sustain?" Each of these small steps can be stacked, and you will get an incredible exponential rise.

For example, doing 1% of your chosen exercise can give you 50% of the results you want.

Ask yourself, "What is the 1% of meditation that can help me get 50% of the mental and spiritual goals I want?"

So again, you are not wired for bad health. You can make small, sustainable and exponential changes to improve your health, while also changing how you think and how you operate yourself. You do not have to be a victim to marketing myths your parents told you, or the subconscious hold that many of these ideas have on you and how you live your life.

The starting point is merely awareness. Start to think about the things you do.

- Why do you eat the way you do?
- Do the things you eat and drink actually provide you with nutrition and sustenance?
- Do you go along with the crowd when you're out and about?

When you start to ask these questions, you can make smaller changes. Instead of stopping in that restaurant everyone is talking about after work, maybe go somewhere you know does proper food. If you do go to eat with friends, don't just order a burger because that is all that your friends see on the menu. Rather than eating three times a day, simply wait until you are hungry.

If you start to tell yourself that these changes are impossible, that you cannot stop wanting to eat some things, or that you are incapable of good health, what you need to do is start to question why you think that. This inspection, and the resulting awareness it provides, is incredibly important.

Proceeding the following action items, these notions bring us effectively into the next chapter, where we will further discuss how to change your thought patterns.

Action Items 4

1. **Create your health vision: what is your main goal? How do you imagine good health? What will it take to get there?**

Think what a healthy person is, and picture yourself in this state of being. Write down what you want to achieve and how you imagine a healthy person, and solidify this in your mind.

2. **For every action you want to do, start asking yourself: does this fit my vision?**

For example, do you want to try a new burger just because your friends told you it was good? Consider if this is what you really want, and ask if it fits within your health vision. Use this mindset for every decision-making process. After each day, reflect on how effective your decisions were. Did you refuse something bad for your health, or do something additional that is good for your health? Take note!

3. **Start validating your own positive decisions, rather than looking for external results.**

If you refused something bad or did something positive, you should be happy with this achievement. Do not look for external validation from other people, whether this be specific weight goals or other targets forced upon you. Even a small change in favour of positive health is a start, for the effects will build up.

4. **Start considering food and drink in relation to life force!**

When you are going to eat something, consider what the food item is, as well as where it is from, and imagine what it might do for you. Is it nutritious? Is it natural? What will it give you?

5. **Remember to do the 1% (80/20 to the 3rd degree) of each activity you want to do to get good results.**

If you are aiming to become more physically active, then think about an activity you can do, even if it is just for a short amount of time, every day. If you are worried about diet, then what is the 1% of your diet that needs a change? What is the 1% of meditation that you need to do to get the results you want? This one activity may get you most of the way in your results. Then it will be easier to just add a little bit more.

Chapter 5

Thinking Beyond The Speed of Light

Throughout this chapter, various ways to change your thought patterns will be introduced, which in turn will allow you to better deal with cravings and negative thoughts.

To begin, I would like you to simply be quiet for a moment and try to clear your thoughts. What do you notice? What is occupying your mind at this moment, and why is there so much stuff? Ponder these questions, as an exercise to build your awareness that there is *nothing* empty about being silent.

In Chapter 2, we touched upon the notion that you are an electromagnetic being. Given this, your thoughts are an aggregate of what is happening in the environment around you, both seen and unseen. All of these thought patterns do not merely occur at the physical or thought level, but also that of the quantum. It is in these instances that you begin to *think beyond the speed of light.*

Applying these ideas to our health, it is when our mind whirs and functions at such high speeds that 'mind loops' can occur, providing obstacles to our coherence and ability to set our focus on achieving our ultimate goals. These mind loops represent the way you think when thoughts repeat themselves, getting in the way of both health and well-being.

How often do you get stuck, telling yourself you can't possibly live without something you know is bad for you? Or tell yourself that you are worthless and always going to be out of shape?

Do you often get caught craving something, unable to think of anything else?

These are mind loops!

These types of thoughts can go round and round in your head. How you think, even if you are not always conscious of these thoughts, can put up near-invisible barriers that prevent you from moving forward. Tell yourself you can't do something enough, and you will believe it.

We need to overcome these mind loops, which is where we can use what I like to refer to as our sixth sense: our vision of ourselves. Don't worry if this concept is new to you, for all will be clear soon.

This chapter will outline how you can break out of negative thought patterns, by utilising a different type of perception, and thus shifting perspective. This will enable you to employ new methods to conceptualise your own self, in order to adjust to your own worldview and aim for better health. You do not have to take every aspect literally, for they should instead be used as psychological models through which to contemplate as you as an individual see fit.

The aim of this chapter is to allow you to come away with an ability to step out of negative thought patterns and take control, or at the very least acquire a basic understanding of this process, which you can then practise to reach your ideal destination. Health is a journey after all, one that we have to embark upon and practice to reap its rewards.

Mind and Reality

As an integral component that forms the basis of this chapter, you need to recognise that there is a difference between your *mind* and *reality*. How you perceive the world is affected by your mind, and therefore the reality you then engage with will change. In other words, if we create an ideal and aim for it, our very reality can change.

If you can only conceive of mediocrity, you will not change your reality. For example, if you cannot imagine or envisage yourself eating better, you will not be able to change that behaviour. However, if you can imagine yourself as a healthy person, who does indeed do the things that fit within your own health vision, you yourself can then create this reality in real life. You can change your reality for the better! This is the very kind of reinforcement that we need to deal with.

In the previous chapter, I explained how you are not wired for bad health, but rather your mind has become hijacked by various tricks and myths. These shape your reality for the worse, yet reshaping this reality in spite of external noise can allow you to create one that is more positive. In order to do this, you need to understand how to change your thought patterns. Your mind up to this point has likely been modified, but you can change it back — for unhealthy mentalities will never be set in stone.

What is Quantum Thinking?

To start with, I will introduce you to the concept of quantum energy — I like to say that it is the smallest, indivisible unit of your energetic self. And what does that mean? Well, you came from your parents, who came from their parents, and so on. And if you go back far enough, you will eventually end up at the beginning of the universe.

So, what existed first? Energy.

Whether you believe in a god — which we might understand as a kind of energy — or that the universe just *is,* there is inherent energy behind all things. Therefore, you are both a form *of* and can be divided *into* energy.

Now, you don't have to accept this literally — that is fine. But it can help you understand what I am talking about here. This can be a conceptual tool to visualise yourself, in order to make substantial changes. It is simply the core idea that all the different small parts of us can work together, to create what we are now.

You are full of different moving parts, right? Muscles, organs, bones, cells and so on. You have different parts of your mind, and of your spirit. Yet these are all guided by *you*. You can guide them in unison and make a change. Quantum thinking, then, is about guiding these small things (which themselves guide you), which may currently be working in the *subconscious,* and making them *conscious*. This will allow you to enter a new mode of operation. This will be expanded upon later, but for now understand that this chapter is about how to think differently, and how to be aware of your thoughts, to beat the things that hold you back. This will enable you to guide both yourself towards your goal, and every part of you towards something better, to break out of old thinking habits. At the same time, you will be shown the path towards directing your thoughts in a certain way, to find the subconscious root of negative thought patterns.

Previously, I referred to the sixth sense, yet you may be wondering what I meant by this. Well, we all have five known senses that engage with the physical world. But have you ever thought about someone, and all of a sudden, they called you? Or perhaps had an overwhelming sense of Deja Vu? Or any other weird, impossible-to-define, moments?

We experience these things, and certainly sense them, but cannot pinpoint them. It is these very types of experiences that are our sixth sense in motion. Whatever you think may be the cause of this, it indicates that there are some things, some capacity for sensing, that may not be fully identified or understood. For ultimately, each of us garner the ability to feel more than the standard senses we are familiar with. This line of thinking also indicates that we have some pretty amazing abilities that we should take better advantage of.

How your sixth sense relates to quantum thinking is that, when we start using both our health vision and our powerful minds to picture and aim towards something, we can employ this sixth sense to then engage with quantum energy. To put it simply, by using a vision to guide ourselves, we can *direct* every small part of us, and become aware of what we do not usually *identify* as part of us. We can then take control of the things that appear to control us. Because *we all* hold everything within ourselves, each and every one of us; all our behaviours, our desires, our feelings. This means that we only need to look inwards for information to improve our health.

Often, we do not identify these thoughts and feelings, this capacity for finding answers within. We look to the world around us and get lost, confused and tricked. Then we end up struggling to make a change, and these old mind loops come back. By turning inward, challenging and changing your thoughts, you can create a reality that you really want. All you have to do is to look within yourself!

To summarise thus far, we need to think with a big picture to direct all the small things within us. Use your way of thinking to get in touch with your subconscious and create a new reality— a crucial step to changing how we think and breaking mind loops. So now, you may ask, what exactly is a mind loop?

Mind Loops, Explained

What do you believe about yourself?

Belief, like all things, is an energetic process. You put energy into having a thought, right? And if you have a thought, you then have a 'loop'. You feed this thought with some energy, so the neurons can connect to create this thought. When you have a disempowering thought, such as "I'm too fat," or, "I can't live without burgers," you are wasting energy that will come back into you and magnify itself.

Then this thought can become reality. Your subconscious repeats it, and your body will obey this thought. For indeed, your subconscious, which listens to these thoughts and may even be where they come from, is incredibly powerful.

From a scientific point of view, while estimates vary, the subconscious brain can process around 500,000 times more information per second than the conscious brain. 11 million bits are sent to your brain, yet the conscious part of it cannot handle all of them. As a result, if your subconscious gets stuck in a loop that suggests you are not worthy, lovable and cannot win, the odds are immediately against you. This is why we have to break these mind loops and feed our subconscious with positive beliefs. This is also why we need to learn to listen to our subconscious, get in touch with it and understand its power over us.

In my sessions, I help my clients get in touch with their subconscious, so that they can better understand themselves. Too frequently, there are so many subconscious issues people are unaware of, processing all these powerful ideas. And while your conscious mind is somewhat aware of their effect, you may not fully identify what the thought is. Your subconscious may be telling you to make a change, or that you are doing something bad. Or, simultaneously, it may be reinforcing some negative thought onto you, without you realising. The thing is, this is all within you! You can listen to your subconscious, and you can change it!

Your belief that, "I can't live without chocolate," (something I dealt with a lot!) or whatever it is you struggle with, may have some deeper subconscious root that we need to get to the bottom of. Your subconscious may tell you this because you were told by your parents that you are too big, and love chocolate, which perhaps defined you. In this case, there is a deeper loop we need to deal with. Yet it is important to remember that it can be dealt with, and you can change how you think.

Without any further delay, let's look at an example of a mind loop and how to come out of it, through the use of quantum thinking.

Getting Out of a Mind Loop

To start, let us say your main issue is that you want to reduce your food intake.

You know that there is one particular food that you cannot get rid of the cravings for — for lack of a better term, in this context, an addiction. You dream of this food and cannot picture yourself without it in your life. You stock up shelves at home, or when you do not have it for a while this food is all you can think about. I'm sure we can all relate to this in some way. And in these cases, we have a mental issue that has a direct *physical* impact on our health.

If you want to be able to not crave certain foods, this intrinsically means that you do currently crave them, right? Because you say, "I don't want to crave this thing any longer." Well, hang on a second. By thinking this, you will have already created a reality that you do crave this food. By admitting this craving, you submit to accepting that this is simply the way the world is. If you say you cannot do anything but crave chocolate, you are tying yourself to this belief and that it is unchangeable.

By always telling yourself you don't need something, or trying to deny the cravings, you are effectively shaping reality, and giving this reality power. Your mind has created this idea, this mind loop, that you crave something, which in turn reinforces a negative reality around you. But it doesn't have to be a fixed reality.

Essentially, to think of a particular thought, you have to allow that loop to exist. So, if you say, "This doesn't affect me," then you first have to think about that particular food and how it has affected you, already. If you say, "Chocolate doesn't affect me," you have literally just imagined chocolate, thought about it and are being impacted by the thought of it. The very act of thinking something doesn't affect you will conversely do so, by creating a reality where this thought influences you. For you will have created this reality in your mind.

If you are addicted to, say, nicotine, one of the things that must be broken in order to quit for good is the need to constantly think about it. If all you can think about is how you are denying yourself that one cigarette, you will still be thinking a lot about it. It will still have a hold over you, thus making it harder to avoid. Of course, nicotine has a physically addictive side to it, and quitting is a process in and of itself, but the point is that thinking about it, even when trying to reassure yourself that you don't need it, can inadvertently recreate the reality that it is important to you. What we want is to stop thinking about it altogether.

The same applies to junk food, whereby too much thinking about and wasting your energy on rejecting it will create this loop. You will have created a reality wherein you crave the cigarette, crave the burger, whatever it is, and your entire being will be directed to accept this reality of such cravings. Instead, we need to direct every cell to a new reality, where these things have no power over us.

Therefore, for a mind loop to not exist, you have to ask yourself: what if you didn't think that thought? What if that thought didn't exist? Where would you be, instead, by releasing yourself from it?

Think of what you generally crave in your life, or a thought you cannot stop having. Ask yourself what would happen if you didn't think about it? What would you be thinking about instead? How would you feel? A lot of different thoughts may start to come up from within you, and you can then begin to get somewhere. All of a sudden, you may realise that you have stopped thinking about whatever it is you crave, and are now getting to something else. Then you can begin to change your thought processes.

For example, if your loop is some negative thought along the lines of, "I will always be unhealthy," try to imagine if you didn't think that way. What would you like to imagine? I cannot tell you, for the answer can only come from within yourself. But the thing is, you will begin to ask why you are even having this thought at all, which will allow some new things to come up. You may then uncover your parent's voice, or some traumatic moment from your childhood, that has been affecting you subconsciously for years.

You can then dissolve the reality that you yourself created. No longer will this thought process, this loop, hold power over you. You will simply stop thinking about it, because you were able to interrupt it.

For a moment, let's take this concept back a little with an example. Imagine I am sitting on the couch, doing work, and think, "Man, I really want a cookie. I'm craving. I'm praying for a cookie."

Then what? Well, I might be craving this cookie, but could ask myself, "Okay, well what if I was able to not think that thought? What if I didn't want a cookie? If I could do this, then I wouldn't be distracted from my work, nor be thinking about the sweet taste of it. But now I do want it, and I'm not sure how not to."

Okay, let's go down the rabbit hole. Which thought do I want to handle? Do I want to handle the sweet taste that I apparently crave by eating the cookie and giving in? Or do I want to handle the fact that I seem to be unable to not want it? Clearly, I have a choice to make.

So, I could then say, "Okay, well let me handle the notion of being unable to not want it." What you need to do is think about *why* you are thinking a certain way. In this situation, I could just think to myself, "What if I decided to just have the cookie? That sounds far easier" If I did so, I would just have the cookie. But I could instead ask myself, "Is having the cookie what I actually want to do?"

In the short-term, yes. I would eat the cookie, and satisfy the craving, but then probably feel bad that I gave in, all the while knowing that I cannot live without gorging myself on cookies. This is of course not what I want to be doing. Because, when considering the long-term, the answer should be no, because it counters my health vision and what I want for myself in the future. Instead, we can go back and handle the reason *why* I want it.

When you handle the first thought, the one that dictates, "I want a cookie," if it is just superficial, it will collapse and dissolve when you start to think about it. This will allow you to no longer think about the cookie, or whatever it is you are craving, when you start asking why you want it. It will then go away, and you will no longer even think things like "I *don't* want a cookie." These thoughts are just as bad, as your brain uses energy thinking about 'cookies'.

When it is not superficial, and you seem to *really* want something, or cannot stop thinking about something, whatever it may be, then after interrupting the first thought, all of the supporting thoughts will come up.

Going back to the cookie example, to make things clear, if the thought of the cookie remains after asking, "What if I didn't feel this way?" What will happen is, instead of thinking, "I want a cookie," other thoughts will come up like, "I wanted to taste this thing in particular." To which I can then ask, "Why? What if I didn't think that thought?" Maybe the answer is, "I want it because I know it feels this way when I have it." Or perhaps if I keep asking these thoughts, I may get to something like, "I want it because I'm currently bored."

And as each thought comes up, you can then handle them one by one with the same approach:

- ***Why do I think this?***
- ***Why am I bored?***
- ***What if that thought didn't exist?***
- ***What if the sweet taste of the cookie didn't exist? What if I imagined a different taste when I eat a cookie?***
- ***What if I ate something savoury?***

For example, you can think, "What if I craved a different taste?" You may think, "If I didn't imagine and crave a sweet taste, then I would probably look at others such as savoury and sour, and want them instead. But I'm not hungry when I think about those, and so don't want them, and thus don't want to eat. Maybe I'm actually thirsty. Ah, okay, I'll have some water." Effectively, in this case, you have gotten to the root feeling, which was thirst.

We can begin to delve deeper into what is going on by simply asking why you think this way, and what would happen if you didn't think like this. These sorts of questions can be a way to take the charge out of each new thought, allowing you to become aware of what your body and mind are really telling you. Maybe you don't crave a cookie, but are simply bored. Maybe you do not think you can't be healthy, but instead have some traumatic childhood memory locked away. I don't know. But you can find out.

As a side note — when you think you are hungry, drink more water. Often, when you think you are hungry, your body is actually saying that it is dehydrated.

However, if you do actually feel hungry, after having learned what *true* hunger is, *especially* when you are using the hourglass model to develop a healthier eating pattern, this is when you really should eat. This signal means that you are not getting enough into yourself. So of course, eat in order to not go hungry. Back to the topic at hand, however. What happens is that when you take that thought, and then you decide to remove it, you create space in your mind. And in that space, all of the other things are possible. Some other thoughts may come up, but eventually you will be able to remove them and create a new reality that isn't clouded by them.

What about thoughts of a more negative nature than just cravings? The ones telling you that you can't change? Or that you are not worthy of success? They can also be loops, and we can struggle with them. Even when we try to put them out of our minds, we often still exert energy on them. The important thing to realise is that, a lot of the time, when we trace these negative thoughts, we can find where they come from, and then try to make a change.

I once had a patient who explained how he was a negative person, with negative thoughts all day. These thoughts were automatic, so from his perspective nothing triggered them, they were just always in the background. I asked him whether he had considered that something could be entering his thoughts subconsciously, yet he said he had never thought about it that way.

To respond, I used the exact same approach we went through just now. I first asked him to imagine if he could try not to have those negative thoughts. At first, he said he couldn't, a reaction that I'm sure you are likely having now. However, after several attempts as he tried to imagine not having negative thoughts, the charge just left. He interrupted these thoughts, trying to imagine not thinking them at all, which allowed the space to open up. Then, because he was no longer in a mind loop that reinforced himself with them, he realised where they came from.

It was his father's voice telling him he was not worthy, something that he had carried around for decades — these thoughts ultimately came from his childhood. As he grew up, he originally thought that he had needed to steal food to live. Yet after our work together, he began to realise that this action was simply done to get noticed, because he did not feel worthy. So this feeling of unworthiness, built upon his father's voice, was carried for years (this man was 60 years old) as a mind loop, holding him back. But once it was broken, his mind was free.

By simply trying to inspect his own thoughts, imagine not having them and question himself, he was able to dig into where these thoughts came from. This ultimately enabled him to begin to take control. This is what I want you to do. It may be tricky at first and will take practice, but you will be amazed at what you can do.

It can be very powerful if you take the time to actually play with these thoughts, because whatever you can come up with will help show what is supporting them inside your mind. And if we remove them one by one, a psychological state will eventually be reached whereby the emotional charge disappears.

This is exactly what you will be able to experience — the emotional charge will drop off, leaving you to contemplate, "Oh, I don't want that anymore." And that simply comes just from questioning your thoughts, one by one.

So, that is how you break a mind loop. You start to ask questions, and eventually find the root cause that is buried in your subconscious. This creates the space to direct yourself, your vision of yourself (which goes back to the sixth sense), and all the parts within you, towards achieving this vision.

The Principles of Breaking Mind Loops

To add to everything we have discussed prior, two principles underpin the ability to break down mind loops:

1. Presence
2. Perspective

90% of the work that goes into the process of asking, "What if I didn't have this thought," is through the practice of presence. This is because you are questioning, "Alright, what is happening now? How do I isolate those thoughts and slow them down?" This embodies what it means to be present — being aware of the moment, and of what you are experiencing. Presence is something that is hard to practise, and is easy to overlook, yet it allows us to better understand ourselves. Too often we end up in survival mode, merely rushing to the next thing. We rarely reflect on what is going on both *around* us and, importantly, *within* us.

I want you to reflect on this all for a moment, then ask yourself: how do I know that I am present? That I am right here, aware of the current moment? The obvious answer that probably comes to mind is, "Well, I am here! I am reading!" Yet, how do you know that you are truly present to the situation?

Is it the way you are breathing, your thought patterns, or a feeling in your body? Think about this, and reflect on how things are moving, both in your body and your feelings. How fast do your eyes move? How fast do you breathe? Are your muscles twitching? Listening to your body allows you to feel a sense of presence. Take a moment to think about what you are doing, as well as every process your body is doing, and attune to the present.

Once you have, we can talk about perspective. Perspective is how you see the world. Things can be close or far, and things can be big or small, depending on your perspective. For indeed, a *different* perspective can, naturally, help you understand things *differently*. When we dealt with the mind loop, all we did was shift the perspective by one degree, just by asking, "What if this thought didn't exist?" So, you were no longer thinking, "I want a cookie," but rather, "Why am I thinking this?" This represents a different perspective of the initial thought, and a different perception of reality. You change your thinking, and your mental perspective.

This will allow you to change how you engage with and understand a thought. All of a sudden, that craving won't seem so big and overwhelming, as you come to understand what it *really* is saying to you. You do not crave a cookie because cookies themselves are so powerful, perhaps you are instead simply bored. You *do not* think you are a failure because *you are* a failure, it is instead maybe your parent's lingering voice in your mind.

When we have presence in addition to perspective, we can change *anything*.

The overriding concept, here, is that if you have enough supportive mental models to fall back upon, then your end results are going to take care of themselves. If you have particular ways of thinking, and those tools are supportive of your outcome, you do not need more. Mind loops, quantum thinking and energy are all components you need to engage with in order to positively modify your thinking. This will allow you to achieve anything, while being healthier physically, mentally and spiritually. Thus far, we have used your mind, your capacity to be present and have perspective, to beat a mind loop of a craving. Effectively, your large vision must guide every part of you to the big picture, while using quantum thinking to beat the mind loop.

Health Visions and How to Realise Them

I now want to touch back upon the idea of a 'health vision', as it itself is a major component of quantum thinking. Thus far, you may feel that what has already been discussed is all well and good for dealing with *thoughts*, but directing yourself to being truly healthier just doesn't seem achievable on a *physical* level. This apprehension relates to mind loops, because similarly to the approach we use to break them, we can also employ a different way of thinking to move past this kind of worry. This will naturally allow your reality to then change, too.

For example, in your own health vision, you may picture yourself as fitter, healthier and able to move with ease. To be in better shape, eating well, hydrated and physically active. But perhaps you also feel that, right now, your body will struggle to be active in these ways. This would certainly be an understandable concern, yet I want to take a moment to immediately address it, and what this type of concern represents. When we are in these situations — of having a vision in our minds, yet our body does not follow or resists — we have to take things gradually. A health vision is not an immediate fix, nor is any of my advice when taken on an individual level, as everything I share is ultimately part of a wider journey. Yet, when combined and considered in unison, this information will guide you, and allow you to use what is already inside you to achieve your goals.

Let's say, in your mind, you constantly desire to be in good physical condition, and use this to guide every part of you. This might inspire you to put aside all the negative thoughts and cravings that get in your way, and take the key steps towards good health, i.e., proper breathing, hydration, food and so on.

Yet what if, after all of this, you still don't look the way you do in your health vision. Naturally, many of us would decide to do some physical activity to help. You might think to yourself, "I'm going to go out running," and add this to your health vision.

But what if you've never run before? If you are overweight, or have a physical condition that makes such an activity impossible?. You may already have this vision, this picture of running, in your mind, convincing it of what you want to do, and why. And yet your body is physically unable to perform. What do you do? Again, in these instances, we must utilise mental models and different practices to change our thought processes. Fortunately, there are multiple ways through which to do this.

The first is to challenge yourself. Your original self-prescribed challenge might have been, "To be healthy I must run," but in the above example, this is impossible to solve. Instead, you can ask yourself, "What is it that I expect as my reality?" The answer at this point has already been established as, "I'm going to go running," right? Well, now you're in a circle. You are expecting something unachievable and unrealistic to become reality.

So, instead, ask yourself, "Is this actually the most supportive option for me?" Now you can go through the logic to arrive at what *would* support your health vision. Most people will decide, "I've decided to run, and therefore I am going to go running." But the question you must actually ask is: "What can I do right now that is both *achievable and good* for my health.

To put it another way, if someone decided that running was the solution to their health problems, but could not physically do it, attempting this activity would have an inverse effect. Indeed, it would be logically contradictory to try to do this exercise, all the while knowing you couldn't. You instead need something that will be good for your health that is actually achievable. Might some lighter exercise be a more realistic option? Perhaps taking a walk might be better for you right now? Think big picture; think long-term.

Another option would be to employ inversions, the technique discussed previously. These can be used in any circumstance, but are particularly effective when implemented if you are struggling to identify appropriate and realistic actions for you and your vision. You can ask yourself, "What would be the worst thing I can do to reach my health vision?" Presumably, the things that will come to mind will be: eat junk food; stay at home the whole day; do as little, physically, as possible, among various other obvious answers.

After moving through this thought process, you will then have a chance to work backwards. Maybe you could start with a little bit of walking. Maybe some exercise, or some healthy food. You have the answers within you, and all it takes to bring them out is to think differently, and shift your perspective.

I hope by now you can see that you have a range of mental tools to help you!

So, if you are in the sort of situation whereby you simply don't know what you can do to take progressive steps towards your health vision, start by asking questions such as, "How can I get healthy without running?" or, "How can I achieve my health vision in a different way?" Then you may find that an answer comes to you. If nothing does straight away, you can then turn to inversion to work things out, by thinking about what you shouldn't do, and working backwards. And why does this work? Because you already have an inkling. Inside you are the answers — some of which may already even be popping into your head at this very moment.

Again, a lot of what this requires is being present. You must take a moment to be aware of what you are thinking, what you want and what is behind your thoughts — this will enable you to change *everything*. Do not decide to run, simply because you can think of no other form of exercise, if you know that this will be harmful to your health. Perhaps this could instead be a goal for the future, and something to build towards.

You could start by doing breathing exercises, hydrating properly, eating well and building up your strength of mind, so that the physical condition holding you back repairs itself, all of which can be done naturally. And then, you can slowly build up, as part of a longer-term, and more well-considered plan.

Your outcome can be the same, regardless of your current physical condition. You *will* achieve your health vision. You *will* hit your goals. You *will* achieve optimal health. But what you must first do is shift your assumptions, and ask, "Does the outcome have to be achieved right now?" *No — it can be later, within whatever timeline that is most realistic and beneficial to you.*

Again, health is a journey!

You may wonder, "Is there something that can support me while I am working towards taking up more vigorous exercise at a later date?" Absolutely. But I don't need to find this answer for you, you will find them by simply asking yourself this very question. The power of you having this conversation with yourself is much more powerful than if I were to simply give you the answers.

If I asked you, "Alright, so have you decided that you want to run?" And you then reply, "Yes, I have."

I may say to you, "Then tell me: what are all of the reasons you think running is going to be good for you?" You may respond with the reasons, but then remember the reality of your situation, at which point we can explore why running is not the option that you want to take. Then after that, you can weigh your choices. I would then ask, "If you weren't able to run, what would you do that would be just as supportive of your end goal?" and you may come up with some surprisingly insightful answers.

It is not as powerful when I simply say it to you, because I'm introducing debates from my own head, not yours. Whereas when you are the person who's asking the question, that is where you will get the most powerful answers, because they will be coming from you. Effectively, you ask yourself these questions, and find the answers which are true for you.

> ***Only you know what is good for you,***
> ***what works for you and***
> ***what is achievable for you.***

Conflict and Inversion

Inversion can also be used to change a different type of mind loop — conflict — which can occur in situations where you have two seemingly contradictory desires. Again, however, you will be amazed at how you can be present and shift perspective to overcome these kinds of conflicts.

Imagine you have two ideas in your head, say, eating chocolate cake and being healthy, which directly conflict upon one another. As a result of this conflict, it can become difficult to know what to do in order to move forward. When making a decision, you will likely oscillate between two thoughts. This can drag you down and make you feel stressed, as you believe that these two ideas cannot coexist.

In this instance, perhaps all you can think about is eating chocolate cake, while unable to reconcile the thought of the cake with that of wanting to be healthy. Your health vision is clashing against your desires, and you feel bad about it. This is an altogether different kind of issue from simply craving.

However, you can make these two thoughts coexist by inverting the associations. What does chocolate cake bring you — pleasure?

But how would eating it make you feel — Guilty? Sad?

In these moments, you must ask: how can I improve my health, while still feeling good? Bring these different emotional charges together.

By inverting and associating different feelings with them, you can also take away these cravings and desires that may be getting in your way.

I am sure that many of us believe that being healthy means feeling good. When you imagine yourself as being healthy, does this make you feel good? Does it bring you a sense of pleasure?

Make these kinds of associations towards health, rather than eating chocolate cake, or whatever unhealthy food it may be. Try to associate negative thoughts of shame and guilt with the cake. Think about how bad you will feel after eating something bad for you, and how good you will feel by refusing something.

Do you feel that saying no to cake is robbing you of some freedom? Well, rather than feeling restricted by denying yourself a cake, think how free you would be if you were healthy, and all of the things this would allow you to do. Doesn't good health bring you more freedom than eating some cake?

This sort of positive reinforcement, through applying these inverted emotions, will help you overcome this clash of thoughts. We all like pleasure, we all like freedom. Yet cake is not what truly brings this feeling, but instead good health. For a moment, I want to tell you about the acronym **SCIEA:**

- Situation
- Cognition
- Interpretation
- Emotion
- Action

Effectively, when a *situation* arises in our lives, our brain produces a *cognitive* thought, which we then *interpret*. This leads to us having an *emotion*, for which we take *action*. In the most simple terms, what this means is that we respond to stimuli.

However, from the moment between a stimulus being introduced and us interpreting it, there is an opportunity, a space, to interject. You can alter the path of how you react.

So, let's think once more about chocolate cake, and place ourselves in a situation where we are offered a slice. You may interpret this a certain way, whereby accepting sounds like a great idea. But this is subjective, and exactly what the word suggests: an interpretation. You think chocolate cake equals pleasure, but that is merely an interpretation — it does not have to.

If you love the food so much, craving it yet denying it, you will then begin to resent your decision and feel deprived, which will ultimately leave you more prone to giving in and eating it further down the line.

So, we need to find a way to interject into that thought process, which is again all about awareness. If you think about any situation, and how you react to it, just think: why do I think this? What is causing my response? What is the chain of events?

For after all, you do not have to think the way you do.

Using quantum thinking, interrupting the conversation in your brain, and being aware of the processes you go through to get to the final outcome, will enable you to have a completely different end result. Eventually, it will be entirely automatic, and you can have a different response, where craving that chocolate cake won't be a thought anymore.

This sort of process can really help change your engagement with the world. Focusing on the opposite feelings, and inverting them, can shift your perspective. You will then be able to see the world in a new light, as these thoughts have less of a hold over you.

Everything I have talked about here involves a process of constantly asking questions of yourself. Always challenge what you perceive to be your current reality, and then cross-check that with the end result that you want. If you think, "I am so frustrated right now because I'm so far away from my goal", question this.

Is it absolutely true that you're far away?

Now, you may say to me, "Yes, it is".

But what are you actually doing when you think that way? It makes you frustrated, and then you can't take action.

But what if you didn't, or couldn't, think that way?

What does putting energy into telling yourself you are far away achieve?

Is that how you can make a change? No!

Inspect these thoughts, and change your perspective.

Ask why you think them, and what would happen if you didn't?

If you truly have not done a single thing toward your goal, this is no reason to give up. For you will have the infinite potential of a blank canvas, whereby you can do almost anything to make an immediate, positive change. From starting to breathe properly, or drinking some water. Simply by doing these, you will have made a step.

Or you may realise that you have been taking steps all along. Perhaps you have already increased your water intake and amount of natural food in your diet. Maybe you haven't lost the weight you would have liked to, but have at least begun the process — and we have to start somewhere, right?

You must internalise these types of questions, conversing with yourself so that you can communicate with your subconscious, break these loops and reinforce yourself with positive beliefs. And this all starts with inspecting your thoughts.

One day, I had a patient come in for the first time, telling me that she wanted to find out what she should work on to improve her life. She started talking about a house guest who had overstayed her welcome longer than was agreed, and that she felt guilty about having told her that she had to leave soon. We inspected this guilt thought, realising together that she had often been taken advantage of, and that this had gotten worse as she got older.

Then she realised it was ultimately all about her not knowing who she was anymore. So, we talked through things, and worked on putting the mind in a state where she would respond to her own suggestions, resetting the autonomic nervous system.

The fact we got to question the thoughts behind the emotions and work out things, gave her clarity. She knew what was holding her back. Through inspecting her thoughts, and examining what was inside her, she said her chest felt lighter. You may think, understandably, how can I live my life forever questioning each and everything I do? How can I function if I have long internal conversations with myself every day?

Well, the good news is that, eventually, you won't even think about it. This is just the beginning, but as you move away from the negative mind loops, and the things that have been passed down onto you that hold you back, you can take control and practise new habits for good health. These will then become a part of your routine, second nature so that you do not even have to think about doing them. It will take time, but this will get easier.

It is very heavy to carry things around when we don't know what they are. Regarding this, my key lesson is that inspection is the first step, but also that our subconscious is very powerful. Whether we are talking about a simple food craving or something more emotional, everything is unconscious, and we have to learn to be aware of these thoughts and make changes.

In this chapter, you have begun to think about how to use your quantum energy to overcome a mind loop, and are on the way to shaping a new reality in the direction of the goals you want. The question is now, how do we unpack the subconscious to see where these mind loops come from? What is in us that blocks our goals?

These notions ultimately come down to what shaped your entire subconscious, and in the next chapter we will work on identifying this.

Action Items 5

1. **Next time you crave something, think to yourself, do I really want this?**

This interruption and inspection of your thought will begin to take the charge out of the thought, and new ones will arise.

2. **Then you should ask, what if I didn't think this way?**

What if you didn't crave that cookie? That sugary "drink"? That pizza?

3. **Ask yourself questions about what your body really wants.**

Are you simply hungry for something sweet, or actually hungry, thirsty or bored? How do different responses to your cravings, and your feelings, make you feel? Perhaps the idea of eating something else doesn't excite you, indicating that you are not actually hungry, but that your body is telling you something else.

4. **Use inversion by regularly asking yourself, "What would be the worst thing I could do for my health"**

This will allow you to then work out what is something positive you can do for your health. If eating junk food and staying in bed is the worst thing you can do, what would be the best thing? What would at least be a good thing you can do?

5. **When wanting to make some steps towards being healthy, whether exercise or diet, use inversion to work out what you can actually do.**

Ask questions such as, "If I cannot go running right now, what can I do instead?" or "What would be the worst thing to eat?" You will find that as you ask these questions, you know the answers.

Chapter 6

Your Hidden Iceberg

Throughout this chapter, you will be enabled to better understand and access your subconscious thoughts and behaviours, in order to regain control of your thought processes and steer the ship towards a healthier future.

By this point, you should understand that your mind is full of subconscious thoughts that you need to challenge. That perhaps you are unaware of what you are thinking, and are held back by an abundance of ideas that have been passed on to you. Perhaps you think you can never be healthy, or that you will never be able to get what you really want. I cannot tell you what you need to challenge — these barriers are specific to each and every one of us.

However, it isn't just the negative things. Simple behaviours, beliefs, reactions and thought patterns — they too will be subconsciously influenced. You have been shaped by the world around you, but unconsciously there are plenty of influences that you may have no idea about.

How do you tend to eat dinner? Do you eat at certain times because you think, or have been told, that these are correct? Do you associate certain foods with health?

How do you see water? Is it a necessity in your daily life, or something you only occasionally drink?

All of these behaviours come from somewhere in your life, and have subconscious roots.

So, where do these subconscious attitudes come from though? How can we find out?

After this chapter, you will have built an understanding of how your subconscious has been influenced, its own influence on you as an individual and how to make changes to your subconscious, to direct your entire self to reach higher goals.

Everything you do is for a reason, whether this is how you talk to your colleagues and employees, or how you eat. The reasons you perhaps think you are unable to be healthy and have harmful behaviours in your daily routine are all rooted in what you have learned, the various influences on your life, buried in your subconscious. And while the mind loops previously discussed can be beaten, they also have to be fully understood. Your subconscious absorbs information incredibly fast. You can see an image, and while you may want to ignore it, your subconscious has already processed it. We accumulate a lot of information over time, all the while perhaps not even being aware of it. This can lead to our conscious and subconscious being unaligned.

For example, there may be things that your parents told you that you have consciously rejected. But, subconsciously, they could have been absorbed into and shaped both your way of thinking and way of life. Just like my patient who carried his father's voice for 60 years.

As the title of the chapter suggests, our minds can be thought of as an iceberg — we are aware of the tip of the iceberg, but there is a lot underneath. We all have an iceberg: it is not something inherently good or bad, yet we are rarely aware of the full extent of it. This iceberg is the root cause of many of our behaviours, our thought patterns and the reality we create for ourselves. How you perceive the world is what shapes your reality, remember. So, we need to really go deep to see the extent of the iceberg.

Therefore, the trick is to look into it and see what is shaping the world we live in. Your reality isn't fixed — you can change it, and make a change to how you live. Think back to the previous chapter for a moment, where I said we are all composed of small blocks of energy which aim towards a particular vision, and that your mind has often been hijacked by various influences. Well, to help shape a new reality for yourself, you have to understand the various subconscious influences that are currently shaping your reality.

Your behaviours, your mind loops and any willingness or ability to change, rests in the conscious mind. To make sustainable changes, to defeat these mind loops and stop having them, you need to identify what is underneath your iceberg. Icebergs, in the real world, are formed from ice shelves. They don't just appear. This goes the same for the mind: your icebergs are formed by the people who mould you, by the world that you exist in.

We learn from others, forming in our icebergs the repetition of patterns, which leads to us often repeating the same behaviours. The hidden part of the iceberg is our subconscious, our learned behaviours, our thoughts, and everything we are not aware of. We continue to do the same patterns, to have the same thoughts, because they are buried in our subconscious, in our iceberg.

For example, you might think, "I have to get up extremely early in the morning and work right away," but perhaps this is what your parents told you. And what their parents told them. Now, of course, many jobs require us to get up in the morning, while some of us are naturally inclined to get up early. But, if you have a choice, and you know you are not that productive in the morning, why do you still do this? You are not making your own decision. This is something that was taught to you, and you accept it without really thinking.

What if you rejected this idea, accepting that you are more productive going to bed and waking up later, but at the back of your subconscious mind had a sense of guilt? This would occur because you are subconsciously influenced by your parents' perspective on the world.

To have a pattern in your behaviour right now, all you need is to have experienced something that your younger self interpreted as not supportive. For example, imagine a child at two years old, told to shut up by a parent. They might tell themselves that crying is bad at home, before then at the age of five cry at kindergarten, where their friends tease them. This would mean that they learn that crying is not just bad at home, but in fact something that is socially unacceptable.

Then later, when they experience something they don't like, say between the ages of ten to fifteen years old, they might feel they cannot cry, and instead get angry. They therefore *switch* the emotion, and *function* in anger. Then when this person is an adult, they might wonder why they always get very angry, even at the smallest things. If this was a patient of mine, we would work back through everything to find the root of the problem, this subconscious behaviour that reinforces their mind loops.

What is fascinating is that we don't really have a beginning or end as people. If you go back through a person, we get to their parents, and *their* parents, and *their* parents, and so on. The iceberg in your mind is itself a culmination of many other things. Going back far enough, we will reach the energy at the beginning of time, or the universe. Energy expresses itself through all of us. How we perceive the world, shaped by other people and other influences, ripples out to the universe as well, and we pass on a shared vision of reality.

Think about bad parents. Some try to reject their habits, saying "I will be nothing like *my* parents," but then they end up exactly like them. Why does this happen? Because they were so *consciously* thinking about their parents, yet so *subconsciously* influenced by them, that they end up the same.

However, those who come to recognise the shared reality that has been created and they are in, and reject it, have a better ability to carve a new path. But this is all about having an awareness of the subconscious, and of the reality you are in.

This is similar to the issue of cravings, in that the act of trying to resist something is still an act of you thinking about that particular thing. Yet we need to free the mind totally from thinking about whatever it is you're craving, which requires awareness and inspection so that you can then make changes.

One problem is that infants come into the world in a helpless condition. Their primary need for attachment requires looking for someone to guide them. When they then get guidance and find that they like and appreciate it, this is a form of love. This in turn leads to them constantly requiring assurance and external validation. Adults, to break this cycle, have to begin to question whether this is really them, or is it their parents, their grandparents or whomever?

Essentially, we are formed by many things around us, but are not really aware of them. As I said previously, your conscious mind cannot beat your subconscious mind. Therefore, you need to make specific, significant changes, and become more aware of what is happening.

You will have adopted certain behaviours, for example how you approach food, from the world around you, perhaps your parents' attitude to food, advertising or cultural norms. You may wish to try to change your behaviour, but unless you understand the full extent of your iceberg, thus recognising where you got your attitude from, it will be hard to truly make a meaningful change.

This can apply to many different areas, not just food of course. Finding unconscious issues is a cornerstone of psychological help, and for good reason. But we cannot treat an iceberg unless we know where it came from, which is the first point of contact.

- ***Why do you think the way you do?***
- ***Where did you learn your attitude toward food, drinking and health?***

Once you uncover the reasons behind questions such as these, your room for growth will be unlimited.

Peering into the Depths

When you have a thought, when you behave a certain way or when you feel an emotion, this is likely coming from your subconscious. Given this, you must understand these behaviours and emotions, making them clear and visible. In order to do this, you need to follow them, working out where they are coming from, which will allow you to peer beneath your iceberg, and into your subconscious.

Uncovering the meaning behind a certain feeling is far easier when your body randomly feels a physical pain, as you can question what it reminds you of. Perhaps it reminds you of falling off your bike earlier in the week, which is why you are feeling pain right now. Emotions, however, are harder to track — yet that does not mean it cannot be done! The principle still applies — keep digging into your emotions and behaviours, and you can find your subconscious, which influences and guides you.

The main way to identify where your feelings and thoughts come from is both by following and feeling them. Of course, what we worked on in the last chapter, the importance of asking yourself questions, can help. Yet emotions are another major part of identifying your subconscious. Our thoughts can cause stress, which triggers emotions, and this can then make us enter the maladaptive or adaptive cycles, as discussed previously. So, we need to inspect the feelings that come from thoughts, as much as the thoughts themselves. However, our feelings may often not be clear, and difficult to attribute to any one clear thought. It is this very hidden aspect that we need to work on identifying.

In order to do this, as I briefly touched upon above, you need to inspect your emotions, and follow them. Think about physical pain, for example, which gives you a signal that you can then use to figure out where the sensation is coming from. It is totally the same with emotions. To trace the emotions, you need to feel them fully. If your arm is hurting and you ignore it, perhaps it stops hurting as much, yet this does not allow you to figure out what the pain is trying to tell you. It's the same with feelings!

Do not bury them. Do not ignore them. Embrace them, and ask, "Where is this feeling coming from? Why do I feel this way?" And as you start to think back to where these feelings come from, you can begin to identify your iceberg.

As you contemplate your thoughts, you may find that the events in your childhood have shaped your current thought patters. That your feelings and thoughts around food, again, are shaped by how and what your parents fed you as a child. Maybe you feel certain emotions on a daily basis because of what you were told by your friends growing up. Embrace and follow the feeling, and you can eventually get there. It is, once again, all about building awareness.

The thing is, most people do not like to question their subconscious. But it is important to remember that our subconscious thoughts make our problems feel a million times worse than they actually are. This process is simply about identifying our icebergs, and what is true about ourselves.

Now, I do have an abundance of stories about how this *can* be an uncomfortable process, but each demonstrates why we need to power through. One, for example, involves a patient of mine, who was suicidal. We worked together for several weeks, and even after understanding the problems were mostly in her mind, and that she could, in theory at least, beat them, she still created an 'unsolvable problem' for herself by saying, "What do I do if the only solution to stop how I feel is to end my life?"

The actual issue here was with her words, and how she thought. I told her, "These are the constraints: you are telling yourself that you are in a situation that cannot be changed, and that a way out does not exist. Yet with these constraints that you have placed upon yourself, no one can solve that." Because saying that the only solution was to commit suicide, she gave herself no alternative. It was in her framing of the situation that she felt hopeless. I explained that this was the reason why she was banging her head against the invisible wall.

She created this situation, telling herself there was no solution, which was why she couldn't beat it. This was the very reason, I explained however, that the answer was also within herself. We spent a lot of time talking, and she realised, "I have never challenged those thoughts before." She came to understand that it was better to consider her position not as "I am in the situation," but instead, "I am part of the situation", and that she was not fully in it.

The thing is, this involved her digging deep into her subconscious thoughts. At first, she was apprehensive, stating things like, "You know, I've got a couple of lumps that are more of a medical nature you can look at." But these were a diversion, because we were getting closer to the truth. It was only by confronting her thoughts, her iceberg — the deeply buried thoughts that were shaping how she understood the problem — that she was able to help herself.

Whatever subconscious thing it is we try to get at, it will be uncomfortable at first. Yet as you follow your feelings; as you try to conceptualise things differently; as you change your perspective, you will be able to take away the power of those which hold you back. This will also allow you to uncover other subconscious influences you can at least understand and make visible. For a moment, I want to touch on conceptualising feelings a little more, tying in as it does to some of the most helpful advice I can give. Often, when you feel an emotion, like anger, you think this is *you*. We even say things like, "I am angry." But you must remember that the emotion is just something you experience, not something you are. You can therefore choose to be the anger, or just choose to simply be someone who is experiencing the emotion. This is an excellent way to think about any emotion that bothers you, and how to feel it, without harming others or letting it harm you.

This relates to another patient of mine, who once came to me and said, "What did you do to me? I had such a stressful week, and my partner was amazed I didn't fall to bits!" What we did together was work through all the different things that would allow him to work out his stress. Now, he had a good job, and no money worries, yet was still highly stressed. Yet we uncovered that this all came down to his childhood and the abuse he received, in addition to his mother disowning him when he came out as gay, despite expecting and being used to love from her.

Forgiving his mother allowed him to move on, a testament to the power of forgiveness, but also how residual issues build up and can manifest in stress. Digging into your past can unlock a source of your stress, and once identified, you can respond. By identifying the subconscious influences on my patient, making them visible and taking action, we were able to better equip him to handle his emotions. Now, you may be wondering, but what can I do once I identify the problem? So what if I know my childhood was traumatic? Or if I figure out where some emotions come from? What does that change? If these are your thoughts, you perhaps do not yet realise that being aware is the first, and perhaps most important, step.

I don't know your past, or your influences, but understanding that you have these influences, and beginning to look for them, is a major step toward making changes to enable better health. The importance lies in being able to identify where your behaviours, emotions and thoughts come from, for if you are aware of this subconscious influence, it is easier to challenge, move past and change them. Then they will have this power over you no longer.

If you realise that your feelings towards anything, big or small, are because of something that happened when you were young, the charge within you can be released, and you can handle it better. If your thoughts on a topic are because of something traumatic, and you inspect them, you can get rid of them with more ease. This will take practice, sure, but awareness brings things into the open.

When you realise a voice that tells you that you are always going to be overweight isn't your own, but rather your parents, you will know that this constraint holds no real meaning, and be able to let it go. If you realise that you eat a huge breakfast every day because your mother told you this was important growing up, and she got that from marketing, then you can begin to think if it is really what you want to do. Then you may not feel so compelled to eat a lot, or anything, in the morning, but rather listen to your body and its signals.

Once you dig, you may realise these negative thoughts are because of some horrible voice telling you that you can't do something, are a failure, or whatever, which in fact came from your childhood. This could be a negative attitude inherited from your parents, or something that happened with your friends. This realisation will enable you to change these feelings and conceptions, as you discover that they do not come from your own voice or mind, and can now be let go of, no longer having to carry them around with you.

After establishing the importance of identifying the influence of your subconscious, we can now work on influencing it back! This will allow you to replace the negative thoughts it holds with those you truly want to be guided by, leaving you with nothing to hold you back as you set forth into a brighter future.

Changing your Subconscious and Habits

Identifying your subconscious influences is a fundamental step towards then being able to change and retrain yourself. And in order to do this, to start again with fresh behaviours, you need to provide your subconscious with a new blueprint. This blueprint will alter your behaviours and internal narrative in a sustainable, long-term way, to facilitate positive change in both your mental and physical health.

Currently, your blueprints are based on what you learned from your parents, what they learned from their parents, and so on. This is why people often end up marrying people like their parents, because of the patterns of behaviour that they identify with. And sometimes, when people have this dawning realisation that their partner is like their parent, they can question it and dig into their subconscious.

What we need to be able to do is identify these patterns, and these habits, and create new ones that become a firm part of your iceberg. This way, you will no longer repeat the patterns you want to avoid, specifically those that lead to bad health. It is this very shift in habits that we will now begin to work on.

Habits need to be three things: safe, fun and rewarding. Too often when we try to incorporate a new habit, such as daily exercise, eating certain foods, etc., it can feel foreign, strange and ultimately difficult. So, to make them stick when we get started, we must effectively trick ourselves into adopting them long-term.

One way could be, for example, eating an M&M every time you do a push-up. In your first few sessions, you could do one push-up, and each time have an M&M. Then, after a week, you could reward yourself with an M&M for doing 20 push-ups. Then for doing 50, by which point you will likely realise you don't need the M&M. But, you will have associated push-ups with something you like. It's classic conditioning.

Another way is simply to use your thoughts to make your habits enjoyable and sustainable, a personal example of mine demonstrating this well. I take cold showers. I don't particularly enjoy them, but I use the fear of missing out on their positives to motivate myself. There are many health benefits to cold showers, so I stack them up, and think, "Well, if I don't do this, I'll miss out on good health, a great night's sleep, better sex and a stronger immune system." In a sense, it is similar to the inversion I talked about in the previous chapter, where I said to associate refusing cake with freedom, as health ultimately equals freedom.

You can positively reinforce yourself psychologically for when you experience the cold shower (or whatever it is you are trying to incorporate into your life). For example, rather than focusing on how cold it is, think in the most ridiculously sexy voice, "Oh, this is the coldest shower you've ever taken. You're such a strong person. What a wonderful specimen you are." This will associate the activity with this positive reinforcement, culminating in you excitedly thinking, "Oh yay, cold sexy shower time," not, "Ugh, cold shower time." When you establish these new, positive habits, you form them into your subconscious behaviours, and will soon be incorporating positive health-oriented actions into your routine, no longer acting on old, learned habits.

I want to give a quick side note. I do not recommend cold showers to everyone. But there are documented benefits. For example, they particularly strengthen your immune system. It very much goes against traditional Chinese and some other Asian thinking, which aims at heating you up to 'sweat' things out. This is an illustration that different approaches can be totally opposite, but they can still be valuable. It is healthier to drink hot and room temperature water, which is promoted in much eastern medicine, but it also is healthier to have cold showers.

Let's return now to changing your subconscious. Imagine for a moment that your conscious and subconscious form an old-style ship. Your captain provides the order, and that order is run down to the engine room, which then turns the rudder so that the ship goes in a different direction. When you are aware of your subconscious, you become the captain, able to make a change and give the order to steer yourself in the direction you want. So, how do you gain access to the subconscious?

You need to utilise a gamma brainwave state, which is a state where you are both relaxed yet focused, to open up the subconscious, give it direction and focus on gratitude and love. When you are in this state, you can put new thoughts into your subconscious. You can connect both hemispheres of the brain together, so that you're fully engaged, and then install new programming, whether that be a behaviour, habit, thought, feeling or whatever else that you want to have more of in your life. This way, you can shift the direction you go in. And now, I will now explain how to get into this state.

The Gamma Brainwave State Exercise:

One of the most effective ways to get into the gamma brainwave state is to use Heart Coherent Breathing. I will guide you through just how to do this, step by step:

1. Take one of your hands and place it on your heart, imagining there is a hole in the palm of the hand.
2. Breathe in for the count of six and imagine the breath penetrating the back of your hand, going directly into your heart.
3. As it goes into the heart, visualise your heart expanding from the enriching oxygen, and getting bigger.
4. Breathe out slowly and imagine the air going through the hand, as well as your heart growing and shrinking as you breathe in and out. Breathe in again, and picture it getting stronger.
5. Breathe out and imagine all your stresses, all your tension, leaving the body. Repeat steps 4 and 5 one time.
6. Then as you breathe in for six seconds again, allow the heart to relax, and imagine it filling up with gratitude, retaining this as you then breathe out. Breathe in again and let it contain even more.
7. Each time you now breathe in, let the feeling of gratitude flood your heart and every tension go out through the back of your hand.
8. Repeat step 7 as many times as you would like, before taking one last breath as you breathe in, and feel the

gratitude permeate every part of your heart. As it reaches its maximum capacity, breathe out.

9. As you breathe out, let every negative thought, everything holding you back, leave you through your hand.
10. Open your body, wiggle your toes, and then feel supported as you finish the exercise.
11. By this point, you will be able to suggest to yourself anything and everything that you want. An outcome you want to achieve, affirmations that support your goals, and your long-term vision. This will direct your subconscious to guide you, by installing these thoughts within. Now, you can create whatever future you want to create.

So, why does this work?

Action Items 6

1. *Inspect your thoughts, habits and cravings.*

Where did you learn them? Where do they come from? This can regard small things, such as what food or drink you generally like, all the way to something much bigger, such as why you don't like to feel or express emotions. The first step is simply to ask: why do I do these actions, or feel this way?

2. **Positively reinforce good behaviours, such as cold showers, eating well and drinking water, with your thoughts.**

You can condition yourself, and use subtle tricks to get yourself into better habits. Eventually, you won't even think about them, but as you get started this positive reinforcement is an effective introductory step.

3. **When you feel you cannot make a change, reconsider your relationship with the situation.**

Remember, you are not in the situation, but instead next to it— you can change it. Of course, there are some things we cannot change, but we can control the reality around us, as well as how we perceive the world and then engage with it. The situation is not you.

4. Practise the gamma brainwave state exercise.

Consider what you want to tell yourself; what blueprint you want; what behaviours you want to change; what attitude and reality you want to embody. Use the Heart Coherent Breathing exercise above, and try to direct yourself.

5. Suggest to yourself what you want.

Reinforcement of your goals, particularly through the gamma exercise, will allow you to begin to shape the reality around you and achieve your goals.

Chapter 7

Making The Uncontrollable, Controllable

Built upon and furthering the concepts established prior, this chapter will continue to help you access and control your hidden subconscious signals and desires. This will allow you to better understand yourself, by directing your subconscious in accordance with your conscious desires. And to get this rolling, let's begin with a few questions that will make you start to consider how you currently understand yourself:

- *How often do you sit and listen to your body?*
- *Do you really know the feeling of hunger, thirst and tiredness?*
- *Do you understand your emotions?*
- *Do you just carry on with your day regardless of what you are feeling?*

Each of these indicate the fact that we need to listen to ourselves! In the previous chapter, we explored the issue of the subconscious — how it was formed, and how we can make changes. But it is important that we dig further into how to understand what is hidden. This way you can make real changes!

There is a reason for your iceberg, while its unconscious influence on you, if unexplored, is invisible. Life would be chaotic if you were conscious of everything. I already said how your subconscious has many more thoughts than your conscious mind, and absorbs information thousands of times faster than the conscious mind.

If you were conscious of 5x, 10x or even 20x the amount of thoughts and were to experience all of these thoughts simultaneously, do you think you could function? Unlikely.

However, this also means that things can get buried, which requires us to bring them out to the light, so to speak. If we don't then they stay buried, and we will repeat certain behaviours that we would rather not. So, to make meaningful change, you must start to focus on your unconscious thoughts and behaviours, and make them conscious.

This chapter deals with both the invisible signals your body tells you and the things you do not notice, as well as how to be aware of them, in order to then make changes. You will have already begun to be more aware of the subconscious influences on you, your iceberg and trying to make a change to it. Yet we now need to dive deeper into being aware of the subconscious signals your body is telling you, and taking control of these hidden influences. You need to make the *invisible visible*, and the *un*controllable *controllable*. What this relies on is paying attention to the signals your body gives you. This is exactly what the chapter will help to explain, so you can come away with a better sense of the invisible commands your body is giving you, that you often ignore or misunderstand.

Now, to say 'make the invisible visible, and the uncontrollable controllable' may perhaps sound a little 'fluffy', or abstract. So, let me explain in more depth. What this means is all about focusing and paying attention to things that are just beneath your consciousness. Right now, as you sit reading, you have a million unconscious processes going on.

Focus on your heartbeat for a moment. How fast is it going?

Just by doing this, you have now paid attention to something going on in the background that you most likely were not conscious of before. You will have likely gained some information about it too, thinking along the lines of, "Oh, I can feel my heart, and it's beating at a normal speed," or perhaps it feels fast, slow or any other speed you can identify. I don't know, only you do. You are now likely thinking a lot about your heartbeat, because I directed you towards paying attention to it.

So, it all depends on where we direct our attention and where we can gain information from. But, if you perhaps noticed it was a bit fast, you may think, "Hmm, maybe I am not in as good health as I thought," and can then make an effort to improve your health. Again, awareness is crucial to making changes, and by directing yourself towards the invisible signals your body gives you, you can then identify and implement the necessary response.

Why are Things Hidden from Us?

The mind is very good at making things invisible. And why does it do this? Well, it's efficient! This also creates a consistent reality that does not require examination on a daily basis. If you were aware of each and every process in your body going on at all times, it'd be incredibly overwhelming, and your sense of reality would change in relation to so many variables. To function on a daily basis, you therefore make shortcuts so that you don't have hundreds of different thoughts at any second and make a new reality each day, with innumerable thoughts and information bombarding you.

An additional factor is that, if you are hungry or thirsty, but say, "I'm too busy to deal with this," your body will then put those feelings away, and you can ignore them. Your body will then learn this suppression. On the one hand, this is useful when in survival mode to completely focus on what you are doing, but the danger is that you can repress important signals. Your body will want to tell you something, but has given up. Whatever was prompting the signal will still be there. but you will no longer hear it, and not realise until it is too late. The thing is, when you attune yourself to what your body tells you, you can uncover more, and then respond appropriately when your body is telling you what it needs. The more attuned you become, the more feelings you can understand and contextualise. And as more of the invisible becomes visible again, you can take control of the uncontrollable actions you do all the time.

This relates directly to bad health, because you often don't pay attention to your body until it gets so bad that you can't *not* notice it. When things work, you don't notice. And when we don't inspect these feelings, we will not know how to understand them. Or we just go, "Well, this is how my body is," without questioning it.

Are you feeling some negative emotions, and can't quite work out where they are coming from? Random pains? Feelings of fatigue? These are the sorts of things we just put up with because we think they are totally normal. But, while I cannot tell you the reasons for them, there is likely a signal coming to you from somewhere within trying to alert you, but you have tuned it out.

The thing is, when we start to peel away these layers, getting in touch with our body, and our minds for that matter, we realise more and more about ourselves that has been hidden away. What is buried within you is almost endless, and the more you start to focus on everything your body is doing, the more aware you will be of certain things you had no idea about. There is a whole different layer to you that you are unaware of, and it is there for you to explore!

In a sense, directing your focus to the different signals of your body requires you to tune it, which is a sort of meditation. By focusing on everything we feel in the different areas of our body, and the signals we receive, we can bypass all the usual filters that stop us from feeling them. This allows us to pay attention to the various things our body does, and what it is telling us.

Then, by identifying them, we can start to control them. We can ask ourselves how we can influence these things. Previously described exercises, such as proper breathing and Heart Focused Breathing, can also help you get attuned to your body, and focus on it to enter a meditative state. You can really listen to what your body has to say, and then in turn control what you want it to do. This can help you become more present, and if you then listen to what your body (and your mind) are telling you, you can begin to identify some of these signals.

So what is the main lesson in this chapter? That we need to listen to our bodies.

One of the distinguishing features of being able to handle something is being able to clearly see and identify it. If I threw a ball at you, you could catch it, because you can see it coming towards you. You can work out its speed, how hard or soft it is and so on. Indeed, whenever you have a problem that you can see, you are then better able to know how to deal with it. The problem is that we are often not aware of the invisible things in our lives, and the subconscious effects on us.

Also, we may experience certain feelings, but not know how to identify them properly. If I threw something at you in the dark, you may know something is coming towards you, but not how fast, what size or whether it would be safest to jump out of the way. This is what it is like when we try to understand our bodies. There are signals coming at you, but you have no idea what they are, and thus no means to deal with them. Yet now is the time to change this.

Reconceptualising Feelings

Think back to Chapter 6 for a moment, and the former patient of mine who was suicidal. Part of the solution was reframing how she conceptualised her relationship to her feelings and situation. Well, we all need to do that, because we have lost touch with our subconscious signals, and do not know what we really feel, or how we should react to them. Often we think a feeling is just a part of us, and that we therefore have to respond a certain way. Or perhaps we think it is inescapable. But this is not true! Our feelings are not us, but rather something we feel.

This conception of feelings is really important when it comes to eating. Hunger is not a part of ourselves, but instead something we feel. Yet, because of various influences in your iceberg, your hijacked mind and your lack of understanding, we get the feelings wrong! Do we want to eat or are we hungry? Well, we can go for a month without food. So when you sit craving something, do you really *need* it? When you are hungry at noon, even though you ate breakfast three hours ago, are you really hungry?

We go from knowing *what* we want to eat, and *when*, as babies, to a rigid structure as we grow older. To eat at certain, specific times, all the while completely missing the fact that we trained ourselves to do so. We lose the very purpose of eating for ourselves. Do we do it for pleasure, for routine or for urvival? We have learned and mimicked a method of eating, an attitude to food, not based on what our body actually wants but instead from our environment.

Our body thinks it wants to eat these three meals a day at a rigid time, despite this not being what we necessarily need. And everyone is entirely different.

Then, even when trying to make changes, you may feel you cannot control yourself, because you think this sense of hunger is part of you, rather than a feeling. So, you think you are hungry and that you have to eat, despite the reality. You think you are craving that non-food, too, because you have got so used to eating it — you have misunderstood the signals from your body for so long! You need to lean in and go, "What am I actually feeling?" rather than just reacting and spiralling out of control.

So, there are two things happening here. One, we think that our feelings are something other than feelings. Two, we have stopped paying proper attention to what these feelings really feel like, and what they are telling us. It is no surprise we often get it wrong when it comes to reacting to our signals. Or that we ignore them altogether.

We need to contextualise the feelings we have. By contextualising, we can better control and modify them, and respond appropriately. Rather than eating because you feel a touch of hunger, perhaps you instead need a glass of water. Maybe your bad mood isn't something that is part of you, but rather something that subconsciously bothered you in the morning. If you sit and properly think for a moment, you can work out the root cause, deal with and feel it properly, and move on!

I share with my kids the opportunity to imagine and describe their feelings. When you do this, your body can tell what is really going on. Let's give it a try.

Imagine you have a stomachache. What you should do is describe the pain to yourself: "It feels large, uncomfortable and lumpy." Then you should begin to ask questions, and engage with it:

- "What would happen if I massage it and mould it?"
- "What happens if it becomes soft and squishy?"
- "What happens if I roll it around?"

You may then experience reactions to it that you were not expecting. "Oh, now it becomes part of my body rolling around, and contacts less of my belly." Then, instead of energy bumping into everything, the stomachache just slowly stabilises in a gentle space, meaning that it hurts less.

Then it can grow and provide warmth, rather than taking energy away. Once you have that, you can then ask, "What would I like to do with this feeling?" If it's still uncomfortable, guide it, shrink it down in stages, until it is so small compared to how it used to fit. Then you can get rid of it, by imagining it flowing out through your fingers.

When you do this, you are channelling the power that you are born with. The imagination that we had as children is being reborn, and you can apply it to everything, including any emotion! So, whenever you have some feelings, whether pain, emotions or whatever, the first step is simply to inspect them, try to discover them and work out what your body is really telling you. Remember, your body and mind are connected.

Our bodies and minds give us signals to do something about our feelings! Pay attention to them. And are these signals useless? No! When you feel thirsty, you can do something. Does drinking make that feeling go away? Yes, it does.

What about emotional feelings? Well, imagine you have a nervous breakdown. Maybe that was for a reason. Was your body telling you something? Whatever thoughts you have, you need to pay attention to them. We have to learn what the signals are. When we are talking about food, you should understand whether your desire to eat is actual hunger, or something else. But this awareness can help you address emotional problems, too. If you have some feeling in your mind, something getting at you, lean into it and learn what it wants you to do.

The issue is that we often do not pay attention to our signals, resulting in our body aiming for suboptimal conditions. For example, if your body knows you won't drink 3 litres of water, it will try to work with 1.5 litres. If it knows you won't eat when you're hungry, it may stop trying to tell you. So what you need to do here is engage with these signals, and be aware of them.

Do you feel thirsty? Then drink more water. Do you think you're hungry? Work out if your body is giving you a signal that it's hungry or not. And if you actually feel hungry, eat something your body needs. This process of paying attention to the signals will help you take control and make the *unconscious conscious.*

If you listen to these feelings, you can then understand and take control of them. I want to remind you that often when you think you feel hungry, you are not. Again, you can go days without food, and so often the feeling of hunger is your body telling you to drink water! However, we have been told that this feeling is hunger. So indeed, next time you feel hungry, drink some water. You will be amazed at how often the feeling goes away. When you listen to these signals, see how they respond to different actions, and then you can fully understand what the signal *actually* is.

This applies to every signal your body gives you. Whether it's pain, hunger, cravings or emotions. Taking control, questioning and trying to change them yourself, is the solution. It can take time to work out, and you may make mistakes at first. But actively trying to figure out what these signals are and how to respond correctly will reward your health immeasurably.

Think about sickness, as well. Think about how your body is actually reacting. Investigate your symptoms, while trying to see what your body is doing and what it is telling you. See how it reacts to different responses. Some simple actions may sufficiently alleviate many of your symptoms.

Think about sickness, as well. Think about how your body is actually reacting. Investigate your symptoms, while trying to see what your body is doing and what it is telling you. See how it reacts to different responses. Some simple actions may sufficiently alleviate many of your symptoms.

During COVID-19, so many people stopped going outside to avoid getting sick. But staying indoors all the time is hardly good for your health, either. You need good air, you need to move, you need socialisation. You may have found it difficult to stay inside for so long. In these situations, it is good to inspect your feelings, working out what is missing, and what you can do to remedy them. Of course, if something is not an option, you need to find an alternative.

We can even take this right to the very start of the book, when I asked why you picked it up in the first place. You may have had some signals that were trying to tell you that your health is far from optimal, conscious or not.

I want you to inspect this feeling, this niggling doubt, the random aches and pains you experience or whatever it is that is worrying you. Lean into them as much as possible — see how they react to you trying to engage with them, and work out what alleviates them. If it is something more serious, you should of course consult a professional to take a look.

However, you may realise that if you start taking the steps discussed throughout the book, some of these pains, whether physical or emotional, will begin to go away. But the only way to find this out is if you try to feel and engage with them as much as possible.

If you think this is going to be hard — that even though you feel you know what your body may want, or know yourself, you still cannot escape your bad habits nor achieve good health — then you may feel overwhelmed and stuck. You may be thinking that your feelings are so strong, how could you possibly change them? Don't worry.

People often say things like, "When I'm in that frame of mind, I can't choose any other option," especially regarding for example craving something bad for them, or not doing exercise. You may think that you can't resist the cookie, cannot stop yourself from eating or that getting up and out the door to go for a walk is just not possible — even after taking on board everything I've been talking about.

I want to tell you something. This thought is actually good!

It is good because if you are aware of that frame of mind, that already inherently means you have awareness, and can change it. *You are aware of these thoughts.*

A lot of the thoughts we have we do not even pay attention to. Do you frequently think about breathing? No. You just do it, because it is beneficial and necessary. The problem is that too many people also do things such as eat junk food, drink too little water and have a sedentary life, without even thinking about it.

I urge the sceptics amongst you to try my advice here, as this very scepticism means you are most likely incredibly aware of your thoughts. Too many people don't even question their thoughts or their activities, they just go along with what they've learned in life. Yet your health journey began when you became aware of these very thoughts and feelings that you previously could not escape. So, well done!

My patients who found these approaches most difficult, who were at the worst level, eventually found that they were able to apply this approach — of trying to mould their feelings themselves — to other parts of their lives. I've seen my own patients grow and grow, using my guidance, despite real difficulties. Yet what they come to realise when they go on without me is that they can still do these actions and enact real change. That it was in them all along. And once they realise this, they take responsibility — then the magic happens. Anyone, even if you are incredibly sceptical, or feel, "There is nothing else I can do", you *can* do this.

The ultimate way to make the *un*conscious *conscious,* the *in*visible *visible,* and the *un*controllable *controllable,* is to listen to what your body wants, and be aware of when you are in the mindset that makes you feel as though you, "Can't choose any other option." You need to feel those feelings deeply. Then you can begin to take control and modify them. Essentially, it is a matter of being present, being aware of your body and your feelings, and acting on them. This makes the invisible subconscious cravings visible, and allows you to take control of them.

Action Items 7

1. **Begin to describe every feeling you have.**

Is it a pain? What kind of pain? Is your body asking for something? Is it a negative or positive emotion? How severe? How changeable? What adjectives can you use?

2. **See if you can imagine the feelings differently.**

Can you feel something different? Can you move it? Can you change its size or intensity? Can you at least imagine it as a different size or intensity?

3. **Try to change your thought processes by really inspecting what your body is telling you.**

Do you really feel hunger or thirst? What emotion are you feeling or denying?

4. **Respond to your signals — hunger, thirst and tiredness — appropriately, if you are sure that is what they are.**

See how your signals change when you interact with them. Maybe water makes your hunger go away, for example.

5. **Listen to your body's signals regularly and respond correctly as much as you can.**

Experiment to see how they react to different responses. You will eventually learn how your body actually works and what it is telling you.

Chapter 8

How to Be Right 100% of the Time

Throughout this chapter, you will be taught how to be right *all the time,* based on both your innate intuitive intelligence and use of other critical techniques.

Because indeed, *you can* be right all the time.

You can make the correct decision for your health, whether physical, mental or spiritual, in every instance.

You can find the answer to every question you have about what you need to do.

How?

By using what I described previously as your innate intuitive intelligence. It is an innate capability, which is why it is within you. It is something we are all born with — the desire to ensure that our health is optimal! It is intuitive as you do not have to rationalise it, you just *know* the answers to what is best for you.

Innate intuitive intelligence is the knowledge you have inside you that you have lost touch with. It is the ability to understand what you really want, and what you really need to do. This intuitive intelligence can access all the subconscious signals your body is saying to you. Imagine you are choosing between water and juice. Your body may want water, yet you have forgotten how to understand this signal. You have had your mind hijacked to think sugary juice is good for you, and so choose it instead. But actually, if you got in touch with your innate intuitive intelligence, you would never second guess your decision between drinking water and juice. You would intuitively reach for the water.

The answers to your problems can be solved by yourself. I previously explained how your mind has been hijacked — by marketing, by ideas your parents gave you and so on. This clouds your ability to access your innate intuitive intelligence. I also explained how often we look externally for answers, for guidance, and end up getting conflicting information. And that because we have lost touch with ourselves, we fall for answers which do not work for us. Ultimately, the answers to your questions are within you, and you need to find validation internally. This chapter will explain how you can access your innate intelligence and find ways to always be correct in any situation.

Another example of a patient of mine demonstrates this well. He was very struggling to sleep because he was worried about things such as his roommates judging him for being lazy because he had not worked for two weeks, whether he had forgotten to bring something to his grandma, and so on. As he sat with me, he was fidgeting, clearly nervous.

I asked him, "When you go shopping, do you make a list?" to which he replied, "Yes, of course."
I then asked, "Do you cross each item off as you get them?" Again, he stated, "Yes."

I asked again, "When you cross off the items, and you go home, do you throw away the list?" Yes again.

Finally I asked, "Do you worry about them after that?" This time, however, the answer was, "No."

To this, I questioned, "What if you took your thoughts, and you put them in a mental shopping list, crossing them off one by one?"

In response to this, he went from fidgeting to sitting with a confident, upright, chest-out posture.

Observing this, I said, "You might not realise this, but I've been watching you and you are no longer fidgeting."

As we continued, I questioned, "Look, how do you deal with your thoughts? Well, the only way you can deal with a thought is if it is clear. The only reason they're swirling in your brain is that they're fuzzy, or they're an open loop and do not have an outcome. For example, 'Oh, I need to call my friend.' How are you going to get rid of that shopping list item?"

He replied, "Well, I can pencil it down. I can call him straight away. I can decide that actually."

All he had to do was think of the solution (which he intuitively knew), clarify the thought, and pencil it off. There are many other things we can do to alleviate anxiety, but for him, just thinking clearly and about the solution that he already knew all along, helped him address his worries. While I did guide him there, what I was ultimately doing was helping him to get the answer he had within.

When you take this type of approach, you tap into a new form of intelligence that is innate within you. This is why I do not give you 20 steps for better health, a diet plan or hundreds of different exercises. No. I want you to become aware of your inner processes, learn how to inspect yourself, understand your body and get to the answers within you as to achieving greater health and success. This is why we talk so much about the subconscious — it is the key to finding the answers within you for better health.

Be Present

In relation to being correct all the time, we must also consider the matter of presence. With this in mind, I want to share a story that illuminates how reflection can help you take control and make the right decision.

In a consultation with the same patient referenced above, I told him, "Look, you know you have more control over your own reality than you realise, right? I want you to imagine your car."

He replied, "Yes. Okay, I can imagine my car."

I asked him to tell me about it, describing the brand and colours, stating, "Good. Now I just want you to close your eyes. And then I want you to imagine it to be black and white."

He replied, "But it's not black and white?"

"Yeah, I get it. But just pretend it's black and white." So, indeed, he made it black and white.

I asked him, "What happened?" to which he said, "Well, it doesn't even feel like my car, I don't feel associated with it?"

"Well, isn't that interesting? What if you did that with your thoughts? What if you did that to your feelings that you don't want? If you made them something different? So they do not feel like they are yours?"

He replied, "Oh, I didn't think that I had the option to not have them."

For my patient, the option existed inside him. I didn't tell him how to think about his worries, but instead simply that he had both a choice and the answer to change his worries himself.

Too often in life we are in survival mode, and this affects our decisions. And when people are in survival mode their focus is on what is happening currently. If I do X, to stop feeling Y, I will feel the same as the last time I did X. If I eat, I won't feel hungry, like when I ate before, for example.

Too often we do not see that there are a range of options, instead sometimes feeling that there are none at all. If you are chased by a tiger, you get tunnel vision and see only what is in front of you. Similarly, in today's world, we have been duped into thinking the solution is ahead, when we should have been turning to the feeling, to the hunger, and asking, "What are you exactly?" We obey hunger, to avoid it, when we should be confronting these feelings, and seeing what they can do.

If you can be present in the moment, actively reflect on your thoughts and your feelings and not rush to a way to 'solve' them, then you can prosper in the long run. You can realise what is available to you, the actions you can take, and the answer will appear more clearly.

For example, returning to the juice example, you may instinctively reach for a bottle of juice over water, because it is your unconscious habit. But if you paused for a minute, you may think, "Oh, I don't actually want this sugary juice, I should instead hydrate myself. Oh look, there is some water!"

But if you are not present in the moment, you may do what is not right for you or what you even really wanted deep down. This sort of thinking has big implications beyond just what you drink at lunchtime. You can use this at any moment, for any decision, all the while getting back in touch with your innate intelligence.

Think back to the stress scale in the first chapter. You have to engage with different feelings to get through them, which can overwhelm many people. The trick is to be aware of and feel the feelings, for this will naturally help you move through them. When you are in survival mode, you just go along with these feelings, without ever wondering what you are experiencing, or why, nor if in fact you have the capacity to feel differently.

Now, you may be wondering how this discussion relates to being right in your decisions *all the time*. Well, too often we make the wrong decision, because we do not listen to ourselves. Think fora moment about a lot of the food we eat. We eat non-food items full of sugars, fats and salt, because we have been convinced by marketing ploys that they are desirable. Or we stuff ourselves in the morning because we were told breakfast is the most important meal of the day. Yet if you listen to your thoughts, if you identify the answers to the problems that are within you, you will have a lot more success.

In addition, it is always worth remembering that your emotions, and your mental state, connect to your health. It is for this very reason that being in a good emotional and mental place will provide you with the necessary tools to improve your physical health. Yet if you are constantly in a bad mental condition, experience nothing but negative emotions in this maladaptive state, you will conversely struggle to be physically healthy.

Likewise, if you live a sedentary lifestyle, and do not hydrate or eat properly, you will rarely have good moods, because your cells, the things that make you, will not be looked after. Naturally, therefore, you have to look after your body to have a good mental state, and to be able to think properly in order to find the right answers.

Let's Practise

We can employ a simple example of how you, right now, intuitively know the correct answer to a decision. You have to choose between two carrots:

- Carrot A grew in the meadows of an organic farm, had plenty of sunshine, lots of time outside, great clean water and natural fertiliser that it got from all the decaying matter that was present in soil.

- Carrot B grew on a farm where it was constrained to be planted in rows where everything is tightly packed, and sprayed regularly with artificial fertiliser, pesticides and insecticides.

If you were to imagine them as people, Carrot A would be a free-range person, out in the wild, running around and hunting. Carrot B, on the other hand, would be a person who has been confined in prison, and essentially tortured. You already know that those two people are going to turn out very differently, just as the two carrots are.

You intuitively know that something which has been allowed to grow naturally, without interference, will be better, because you know two people who were treated in such different conditions will, thus, be different. You know the correct answer when you reflect, think and look at the things you know in yourself. Intuitively, then, you should know that naturally grown produce will be better for you. And crucially, you can be correct in all kinds of things when you take this approach.

This analogy also serves as an effective point with regards to mental and physical well-being, and their relationship. If you live in a world of good health, are free to roam and do what you wish, you will be both physically and mentally happier. And of course, the reverse is also true. This should be intuitively obvious. Yet still, many people are content with a lifestyle that obviously makes them neither mentally or physically healthy.

You Can be Stronger than Marketing

You have to train yourself to not be swayed by others, and particularly by marketing. You have an innate intuitive intelligence that can be right 100% of the time, but have lost it. It has become buried under a million things. So, do not expect to be right all the time after reading this chapter, or even this book, alone. It is a process to work on that you will have to master. But, you can get there— there is a version of you that is always right in every decision, and it is one that can exist.

The previous carrot example can also be used to think about how your innate intelligence has been hijacked. Marketing may convince you that Carrot B is better. Perhaps they say that it is cleaner in the store, and less bent, so you associate it with cleanliness and freshness. Or they stick some stickers or luxury-style packaging over it, trying to pass it off as good for you under the veil of naturality.

But if you observe it closer and figure out where it is from, you may actually uncover that these sentiments are lies.

Let me give you an example of how marketing has particularly hacked our ability to make the right decisions. When I used to go to the supermarket with my daughters when they were younger, they would ask, "Can I have this? And this? Oh, I also want this!" requests I am sure those of you who are parents will recognise. They were not just doing that because they were kids, though. The supermarket is designed to provoke these reactions, as is the marketing for the products. So kids bombard their parents with questions, and plant the idea in their minds that these products are good. Or they just give in.

Even the layout of supermarkets is designed for you to buy more than you should, the things you do not need at all. These stores spend thousands on design and hiring consultants, which makes a huge difference in sales. It is a profession to design the layout that will induce maximum purchasing. It is all about putting things in your line of vision, distracting you and pulling your attention to the things you don't need. How many times do you go into a store and end up buying way more than you intended? You may think, "Oh, I just remembered that I needed it." But honestly, how many times did you just buy on impulse because you saw it?

Some people are aware of these tricks to a degree, suggesting things like, "Go straight to the back of the store," or, "Don't walk down the middle aisles." Now, on one hand, it is good advice to avoid the aisles containing non-foods, and where you don't need things. To focus on fresh, natural food items, and get out. Sure, to an extent this is a good way to not let these non-food items enter your mind whatsoever.

However, these supermarkets know that people know this! This is why they design these layouts so that you have to walk down certain aisles. They are tracking the flow of customers, and making sure you go a certain way. Now, this is not a conspiracy to destroy your health, but it is a side effect of our society's profit motive.

So, you see, the odds are stacked against you to be right all the time. Yet here is some advice to you parents out there, which I used to practise with my daughters. I would not say 'no' to them when they wanted me to get something — they would simply yell back, "I want this, I want this!" And why do this? Because denying something makes it more appealing, something you cannot stop thinking about. I wanted my daughters to make up their own minds, and learn for themselves. If it was me simply stating that these foods were bad for them, they would not understand why.

Instead, I would say to them, "Okay, let's see what is in it," and start reading all the ingredients. And I mean read *each* and *every* ingredient. And as I read, their faces would change as they got increasingly less excited. Once I finished, I would ask them if they still wanted it, and, of course, they would say no. Picture the back label of some junk food, or maybe even grab something close to hand in your home. When you read everything in it, is that *really* what you want in your body?

Labels can be useful to learn about what you are putting in yourself. So often when you look at packaging, you can discover a lot. For example, a 'regular' can of soda/soft drink contains so much sugar. Now, recommended amounts of sugar vary, but for the sake of understanding this point, the American Heart Association's daily recommendation is 24 grams for women and 36 for men — about 6–9 teaspoons.

How much does an average soda/soft drink can contain? 44 grams! That is twice the recommended amount for women, in just one can. Check out fruit juice as well, which is often just concentrated fructose sugar. Indeed, sugar can be hidden in many things — even in wasabi for sushi!

Now, of course I am not merely suggesting that you read the labels to decide what is good for you, but they can provide information. Even still, you must begin to realise that you do not need things such as labels to decide what is healthy. This is exactly what we have been talking about: you intuitively and innately know these things!

Plenty of labels try to pretend something is healthy, another marketing trick. Supermarkets aren't putting food in there because it's good for you, but rather because they are a business, and the products sell. Carrot B could try to pretend it's healthy with its packaging, but Carrot A is actually the one you want!

A so-called 'health bar' may sell something to you as 'keto', just because it contains a mere two grams of carbs. But that, again, does not mean it actually is good for you. All kinds of terrible things can be in the ingredients. The same applies to things that say they are gluten-free or organic. These types of buzzwords do not mean there are no other unnatural things occurring in the manufacturing process, or that the product is inherently good for you.

Ultimately, you have to trust your judgement. But if you begin to think about what is inside something, and what you are actually consuming, these types of thought processes will go a long way to restoring your intuition. Intuitively, you do not want to eat these chemicals, preservatives, colours or whatever else is in these non-food items. Intuitively, you instead want fresh food items. If you can reflect on this and move forward with a sense of awareness whenever you go shopping, or even just think about food, the better you will be at making these accurate decisions.

Be in Touch with your Baseline

Returning to the hourglass model in the third chapter, establishing your healthy baseline and knowing what is good for you will allow you to always make the right decisions. For one person, eating product X might react fine and be good for their health. But for another, it could provoke an entirely different reaction. Only you can know this by seeing how something reacts with your body, once you have established your baseline. Then, as you begin to know and understand this, you will habitually make the correct dietary decisions, specific to you, regarding what you purchase, eat and drink.

This baseline can apply to your emotions, too. You may understand certain activities make you feel negative, while others in fact fulfil your needs in certain ways. You might also come to understand that you need to do certain things to stay in the adaptive cycle. When you see how different things affect both your body and your mind, you can then know, internally, what decisions to make in your life.

Be in Touch with your Health Vision

You should also consult your health vision to find the right answer. As previously discussed, the aim is to construct this vision, the outcome of which you know is good for you. From this, you can direct all parts of you towards achieving it, and it can guide you in decision-making processes. When you need to pick between two items at the supermarket, for example, which one fits your health vision?

Is exercising, at least even a little, better than sitting on the couch all day? You may want to sit at home, but does this align with your goals? No. Do you really want to do nothing, or do you maybe just not want to go running? There are a range of options open and available to you to do exercise. You must think about what aligns with your vision. Be present, think big picture, and ask *yourself* what fits *your* vision.

At the same time, there is always room to use inversion when you have to make decisions about what you want to do. Which item is worse? What activity is the most at odds with your health vision? What would be the worst thing to do? This you can easily find out, and reverse engineer your own strategy!

At the end of the day, it all comes down to you. And only once you realise this can you be correct in your own approach to better health. Do what is right for you when you discover your baseline, as well as the messages that your body tells you, and know what your body wants by responding. Only you are going to heal yourself. For after all, you are the one, biologically speaking, who replaces your cells. At the end of the day, when you want to repair yourself, it is you doing the repairing. Thus, we have to look inwards.

Let's take stress as an example. Someone may say, "I am stressed because of my partner." I could merely say to them, "You have nothing to stress about. You have a great life, and they love you very much, so stop worrying." But that would of course not be an effective countermeasure — they will continue to be stressed. But, if they have this conversation internally, if they understand that there is no real reason underpinning this emotion, then they can overcome it. It may not be easy, but it has to be from within. This is exactly the same with physical health. You have to have the internal conversation, the internal drive, and listen to your internal voices and signals to apply yourself to the world you engage with.

I said at the start of this chapter that you can be right all the time. And I mean this in every decision you make. Do you need to make a big business decision? Do you need to choose between, say, staying at the office a bit longer or heading home? You probably know, it's just that your decision-making capacities have been hijacked by a lot of externalities. Taking a moment to reflect, to take control, will show you how to come to the right answer.

Yet how do you know if you are making the right choice? What is 'right' or 'correct'?

This is a good question. But what we are ultimately talking about is what is right for you. Right for your health, on every level. For example, choosing to go home and spend time with your family is good for your mental and spiritual health, and you are more likely to get to bed on time. Deep down, you know this, and your subconscious has always sent you the signals indicating as much. It is just that you, with your entrepreneurial mindset, have been filled with ideas about working until the last minute. But this is not always the right decision, especially long-term. Within you, within your mind, are the right answers. I cannot decide what the specifics of your actions should be — *only you* can intuitively know what is best for you.

Remember this. You are the only one who will know when you are experiencing optimal health. You will feel it — no one else will. And when you start to eliminate bad things from your life, when you make routines and feel that you are at a good level of health, then you can understand what is good for you, and make decisions to maintain it. This is how you can be right all the time, because *you* know *yourself.* Consult yourself and you will be right, always.

You have the answers inside you, and you can test your decisions with your innate intuitive knowledge. Next time you have to make a decision, whether about the food you eat, or if you should stay at work late or go home to your family, listen to what you already know. Test what you find against your decision, and you can be right 100% of the time.

Now, however, you need to identify the things that get in your way of making the right decisions, the things buried in you.

Action Items 8

1. **Consider your reactions to any situation, take a pause and be aware of what is going on.**

This can help you leave survival mode, making better decisions.

2. **When faced with a choice, don't look ahead for the answer, but consult yourself.**

You often know internally what the answer is. Try to listen to yourself. Is eating this junk food really good for you? You know it's not! This isn't just about physical health, but any situation, because you know the answer!

3. **When overwhelmed, take each thought and cross them off one by one with what you need to do.**

This is an excellent way to stop panicking, leave survival mode and deal with the issues you face.

4. **Stop looking for answers from outside sources.**

Your knowledge of what is good for you is unique and only applies to you. Therefore, you have to understand what is good for you.

5. **Practice making decisions in relation to your health vision, and your internal knowledge.**

You will make mistakes at first. You will not get it right all the time when you start, because you have lost the ability to listen to your voice. But the more you practise, and the more you try to listen to your inner knowledge, and the more effective you will be.

Chapter 9

Killing Mind Worms

To conclude Part 2, this chapter will introduce the most effective ways to get rid of the buried memories and thoughts that hold us back.

Ask yourself this: do you ever have negative thoughts? Do you feel that some things are just not realistic for you? Do you doubt your ability to be healthier?

You now know you can consult yourself for the answer and be right all the time. We have already covered a lot about what can make health seem a difficult thing to achieve, such as the workings of your subconscious, the things that make you and the hidden factors that influence your behaviour. And now, we turn to one more chapter that relates to the subconscious, containing the final step to remove the negative thoughts it stores that hold you back. Consider it as a wrap up of this section, where we bring everything learned thus far together.

As an entrepreneur, you have likely achieved a lot in your life. Yet even so, we can all have these negative thoughts, many of which are likely held within your subconscious. Even if you are highly successful, you may still feel, deep down, unhappy; that you cannot do something; that you will never amount to anything; that you are destined to fail. What's more, you may not even realise it. This is okay, and is what we are going to deal with. We need to finally get rid of these thoughts, in order to achieve optimal health, in all facets of life!

There are things buried in your subconscious that are part of why you make mistakes, whether this regards eating, work, exercise — the list goes on. I call these things 'mind worms'. And in this chapter, we will learn how to kill them, using everything that we have gone through up to this point: inspecting ourselves, gaining awareness and controlling the uncontrollable.

We all inherit mind worms, maybe from our upbringing, trauma or general experiences, which build up and shape how we understand the world. In a sense, they are an analogy for the deep inner thoughts we are not aware of, and can hold us back. I previously mentioned the iceberg, which is about you as a whole — your conscious and unconscious — and finding the hidden aspects of you.

Mind worms, on the other hand, are thoughts and beliefs that are throughout you, affecting and holding you back, but also removable and changeable. It is another conceptual tool to help change your subconscious.

We have already touched on this topic to an extent when dealing with mind loops, and bringing things out from the unconscious to the conscious. However, what I aim to give are highly successful, you may still feel, deep down, unhappy; that you cannot do something; that you will never amount to anything; that you are destined to fail. What's more, you may not even realise it. This is okay, and is what we are going to deal with. We need to finally get rid of these thoughts, in order to achieve optimal health, in all facets of life!

There are things buried in your subconscious that are part of why you make mistakes, whether this regard eating, work, exercise — the list goes on. I call these things 'mind worms'. And in this chapter, we will learn how to kill them, using everything that we have gone through up to this point: inspecting ourselves, gaining awareness and controlling the uncontrollable.

We all inherit mind worms, maybe from our upbringing, trauma or general experiences, which build up and shape how we understand the world. In a sense, they are an analogy for the deep inner thoughts we are not aware of and can hold us back. I previously mentioned the iceberg, which is about you as a whole — your conscious and unconscious — and finding the hidden aspects of you.

Mind worms, on the other hand, are thoughts and beliefs that are throughout you, affecting and holding you back, but also removable and changeable. It is another conceptual tool to help change your subconscious.

We have already touched on this topic to an extent when dealing with mind loops and bringing things out from the unconscious to the conscious. However, what I aim to give you in this chapter concerns more the ability to deal with these beliefs that hold you back. This will be a final conceptual tool to understand yourself.

This chapter's question is:

- *What do mind worms do to us?*

Do they eat the seeds of our fruit, stopping us from living a fulfilling life? Well, many mind worms can be understood as the limiting beliefs we have that stop us from reaching our potential. It may be some thought like, "I'm too old,' or, 'I'm too fat," or anything that is blocking you in some way.

Picture yourself preparing an apple to eat, one that was grown in your own garden. You picked it, and took it in. It looks beautiful. Then imagine you bit into it and it's tasteless. You think, "Oh no, that's not good. I've got to get rid of it." You throw the apple away, and go and get another from the tree, and yet it's the same — completely tasteless.

So, you look at the tree, and it looks perfectly healthy. You then must start questioning where this tree is getting its nutrients, and the answer lies in the soil. So, indeed, you start to dig into the soil, and realise worms are destroying the roots. Given this, the tree isn't getting the nutrients it needs, which is causing the apples to be tasteless. Yet when you clear the worms and ensure the tree is getting the nutrients, in the next season your apples will be how you want and are meant to be!

From this analogy, we can understand that you have to dig into your subconscious to see where these mind worms are, and what is getting in the way of you achieving what you want to. Your behaviours, and your thought processes, are like the fruit, the result of the entire tree's ecosystem. In the roots are worms, which are the subconscious limiting the beliefs that you carry with you. They are depriving you both of nutrients and of the ability to succeed.

Yet worms can also provide nutrition to the soil. So, we need to kill the bad ones, and ensure that the worms, the beliefs we have, are giving us 'nutrition', rather than destroying everything good. This, in turn, will allow us to have better 'fruit', or rather, a better life.

If you think that you are 'wired for bad health', as we discussed earlier, this may be because of these mind worms. Something that you inherited in your childhood, for example. Perhaps you feel that you have something rooted within you, that is unresolvable. But as with everything we have explored together thus far, this is totally changeable!

Modifying Memories and Associations

Some of these mind worms can be caused by trauma. Previously I talked about mind loops and our subconsciously learned behaviours. Often we try to only deal with the symptoms, or simply ignore them. But ignoring something we know is there requires you to still be somewhat aware of its presence. While there are plenty of things you may not be fully aware of, the act of deliberately avoiding something intrinsically means that you hold some awareness of it within you.

To better deal with it, though, you have to be aware of it, and bring it to the front. For example, with my patients, we often peel away layers to reveal an inner child who is wounded and needs something. And once we can find them, we can give them what they need.

There may be different versions of you to talk to, looking back to, say, your child or adolescent self. These are all important parts of you that may need engaging with to help deal with traumatic memories. Ultimately, you must synthesise these different parts of yourself, in order to deal with these challenges.

Trauma can be severe. I have a patient who was an army veteran, who described a lot of very gruesome images and was always replaying the same nightmare in his mind, over and over again. Of being in the war and having to raise his gun, shoot and kill someone. He was re-watching his actual comrade being blown up into pieces, with his brain and physical body parts splattered all over his face. However, even trauma this severe can be addressed. These mind worms can be dealt with.

By simply utilising perspective, and being able to shift it, he was able to help himself. What I did was take the image, and explain that he had the ability to manipulate it.

For example, I would say, "Try to see the picture. This will mean that you can move in, distort and change it."

As he did so, and with the understanding that he was in this particular moment as he pictured it, I said, "What music is playing in the background?"

He replied, "There is no music." Yet when he sat down and thought about this, he said, "Oh, there really is background music. It's not *Rocky*, but it's a similar sort of building music, like when you're going to go into battle. Oh, that's funny. I never noticed that was there before."

This indicated that the memory wasn't entirely accurate or real, and could be changed. Then he was able to dismantle it.

I said, "Why don't you make it, you know, 'Twinkle, Twinkle, Little Star', and let's see how that affects it."

After doing this, he was able to choose a song that allowed him to go, "Wow, this is stupid." Then, rather than the scary image he usually focused on, he was able to take the charge out of it. Once he gained the ability to manipulate that image, he no longer saw it the same way. So, there are lots of methods that we can employ, such as this, to help with trauma.

I want to take a moment to explain the power of the subconscious once more, so you can see its potential in dealing with painful memories and mental associations that are holding you back. The following passage will provide you with an exercise that can drive home how powerful your subconscious is.

When they hear a word, for example lemon, most people would just picture some unspecific lemon, with no major characteristics or emotional charge. But we are going to try something.

Imagine a lemon in front of you, one that is about the size of your hand. Imagine you are holding it.

Notice its weight, the specific shade of yellow and the dimpling in the skin. Really imagine it in front of you, and take a pause to do so if you need.

Next, I want you to imagine you have a knife, and slice it. Think how it feels as it goes through the first layer, and into its flesh. Then how it smells: can you feel that zesty scent entering your nose? Now, imagine you squeeze it, and the juices run down your hand, along your arm to your elbow, and drip to the floor. Then look at it, look at the seeds in the lemon. Now take a bite.

How vividly did you imagine any of that? The taste, the smell, the sight, the weight. You may have even created some saliva as a response. None of that was real — it was all in your mind. Yet your mind cannot tell the difference between reality and imagination. It does not have to be a vivid 4K, technicolour visualisation. But still, the act of imagining and suggesting can really influence you. But it means it can be changed too, that you can suggest things to yourself to change your own imagination and reality.

And how can this help you be healthier in other ways? Well, imagine you want to eat vegetables more often. Yet you do not like them; they do not appeal to you. How could you make them appealing in your mind? Think for a moment about what sort of tastes, smells and textures appeal to you in food. Try to identify them and associate them with healthy foods.

You may think, "I want to taste something smooth and chocolatey, like a lava cake." Now, take that sensation and try to associate it with vegetables. In your mind, right now, you are likely thinking, "No vegetable tastes like that." But try to work on this connection. By creating positive associations in your mind by visualising, you can, in a sense, condition yourself mentally to enjoy something in a different way.

Also, try to associate these things which are bad for you with those that are negative. Imagine you have an old sock that you wore for five days in the height of summer, and you squeezed the sweat onto the cake. How tempting is that cake to you now? Horrible, right?

This can be a simple, and brutal, but altogether incredibly effective way to take away these charges. At the end of the day, our perception of different foods is merely built via the way our minds interpret and engage with them. Therefore, you have the ability to change the reality you experience when interacting with them.

Visceral sensations are incredibly powerful. Linking together different thoughts can help you move along with shaping a new reality, one in which you can achieve your health vision. Additionally, by taking the time to think and reflect on your relationship with certain foods, or whatever else it could be, you will begin to take apart these thoughts, and build awareness too.

Returning to trauma, the point is that the memories that often shape us and give us issues can be changed. You can go back, change them, so that they are no longer as powerful. Whether it is something like your parents yelling at you, making you cry as you are force-fed some vegetables, that shaped your relationship with food, all the way to more problematic emotions experienced during a horrible event on a battlefield, you can change your memories. This is the key thing to remember when dealing with mind worms.

Finding the Worms is the Biggest Step

Food and healthy habits are one thing, but do you recall how I stressed how important it is to release emotions, just like you release toxins? Negative mind worms are no different. Too often when we avoid trauma, we avoid these mind worms. Yet when we succumb to our natural urge to not respond to trauma, it stays within us. When it isn't released, our mind worms multiply. Therefore, these mind worms need to be confronted straight on.

We must feel and identify our feelings, just like we do our mind worms. By doing this, we can then recognise the root cause of our issues. What the trauma is for you I cannot tell you, but you have to lean into yourself and work *with* it.

As I said, these mind worms come from all sorts of events: our upbringing, our formative years or more recently in our lives. They shape us and our behaviours, whether we are talking about what we eat or even severe PTSD.

When you feel these thoughts, you cannot simply ignore them, but rather feel them, follow them, and work out where they are coming from. By making these unconscious mind worms conscious, and being aware of them, you can take the next step of challenging them. This is how you can kill your mind worms, and stop being limited by them.

When you identify these worms, no matter how severe and harmful they are to think about, try to control these memories.

Change your perspective on what you think as a result of identifying them, shape the thought differently and take away the charge from them. You will then be able to overcome their hold on you. This way, your 'apples will not have worms, because your 'tree does not either. Don't let them burrow away: find and deal with them at the source.

Remember back to the emotional scale in Chapter 3, through which I explained the different emotional states and the scale that stress takes you along. This demonstrated that when we feel our emotions, we release them. We have to go back through ourselves, and feel everything we can, thereby strengthening our level of consciousness.

There was a psychiatrist in the UK, David Hawkins, who examined the levels of consciousness through muscle testing. There is a critical level of emotion when you are in anger, despair, hate, agony and forgiveness.

Now, a quick lesson here is that forgiveness is the best way to resolve a situation with someone else. But you also have to forgive yourself sometimes. When we deal with these negative past emotions, forgiveness can help us release them, move forward and experience higher modes of being. Then you can enter back into the adaptive cycle and have better emotions.

Returning this discussion to the matter of mind worms, by going through our past — examining who we are, feeling it, releasing things and forgiving ourselves — we can go beyond and control who we want to be. A running theme of this book has been bringing things out and identifying those hidden within you. Doing so allows you to modify them. And by modifying, challenging and inspecting your memories, you will be able to take the charge away from them.

Once you identify where something is from, you may often find it has already lost a lot of its power. For ultimately, awareness is the key.

When you identify a mind worm, inspect it as much as possible. Ask questions, and have a conversation with yourself about it, utilising everything we have gone through in the previous chapters.

Ask:

- *What would happen if you didn't think this way?*
- *What would happen if you removed that thought?*
- *What about if you modify the memory?*
- *Who is actually saying this? Is it your voice?*

If not, get rid of it because you should be listening to yourself!

And finally, combining each of these concerns, ask yourself if this thought is something that is in line with the vision of who you want to be. These sorts of questions and conversations will go a long way to killing these mind worms.

Also, remember that you can modify memories. Ways to do this include adding or taking away the music within them, changing the colours, or even completely breaking it down to a point where itis no longer painful or has a hold over you. Do you remember your parents yelling at you for not finishing your dinner as a child? Change the memory and make it humorous; you may find that you no longer desire to always stuff yourself at dinner time.

Examining, identifying and then removing the mind worms allows you to move forward. Question every thought and feeling you have. Forgive yourself, forgive others, feel emotions deeply and employ quantum thinking to remove these thoughts, as well. You do not have to dwell on these thoughts, for you can instead move past them. When you identify where they come from, you can then deal with them one by one, and soon enough you will be free of these worms.

This again illustrates the link between the mind and body. Without being able to examine the worms that are within your subconscious, and the negative memories that hold you back, you cannot achieve good health. Your body is guided by your thoughts, which are shaped by your subconscious, for better or worse. Given this, your mental blockages are what determines your approach to health. So, we naturally have to deal with them to be able to take the steps to become healthier.

In short, pausing, reflecting, digging and getting in touch with your subconscious, while trying to reform your thoughts and memories, can go a long way to getting rid of these limiting beliefs. By doing this, your tree will be pure, receiving the nutrients you want, and you will thrive!

This is ultimately what the entirety of this material is all about: not just surviving, nor just being a bit healthier, but thriving.

Consider how I discussed that spiritual health is about your direction. This is exactly what we need to achieve, and getting rid of these beliefs is a significant part of that. Synchronising the physical steps of breathing and drinking, with the subconscious inspections of the last few chapters, will then allow you to guide yourself in the direction you want. You will not even have to force it, for it will soon become easy!

Action Items 9

1. **Next time you feel doubt about your health goals, ask yourself, "Why do I feel this way?"**

This can begin the process of 'peeling the onion' and finding the origins of these thoughts.

2. **Dig into your memories, and your subconscious, and work out why you feel the ways you do.**

Now, this can be hard — few will enjoy this process. But by doing so, you will be able to identify the issues buried in you and take control.

3. **When you identify bad memories, inspect them and see how real they are.**

Is the memory real? It is important to remember that our memories are very unreliable; you probably changed them from what really happened. Try to identify what you have placed in the memories yourself. Ask yourself whether there is music, for example, or if anything seems a little surreal. Try to see what doesn't seem right.

4. **Take the traumatic memories and modify them to make them less powerful.**

Change the music, the colours, whatever you can. You will see how unreal it is, allowing you to work through them.

5. **Shape your thoughts to be different, by modifying them.**

If you are aware of the mind worms, you can begin to change them. Then you can take control! If you tell yourself to think differently, you will feed yourself limitations, such as, "I can't be healthy, I can't eat healthily, I can't exercise," no longer.

Part 3

Your Own Health Plan

This last section is all about ACTION! We are here to put everything together and make a sustainable plan. You have now nearly reached the final steps that will allow you to embark upon your health journey, so I won't delay any more than we need to!

Join me as you gain the final tools to reach forward into the future in ways, until now, you never knew possible.

Chapter 10

Finding Your Personal Optimal Health Plan

If at this stage, after considering all of the information that has come before, you are thinking, "This is all good, but what do I do? How can I make it last?" Well, this is now what we are here to talk about. Most people know what's bad for them. I know that you can figure out what you need to do to be healthier. But knowing it isn't enough.

So, what is the solution? What is missing? ACTION!

Consistent, stackable, sustainable action. What I call C.S.S. You have so far likely been unable to develop a C.S.S habit that is automatic. I explained in the first section of the book the core concept of health, and how to get there. Then we dived into the matter of the subconscious, to help move past these ideas that hold us back, and how to attune ourselves to our body and subconscious in order to achieve optimal health. Now, however, it is time for you to take action, and move on with the ideas we have talked about. This book outlined many ideas, most of which are simple and easily implementable, highlighting; the importance of being aware of the things inside you; listening to your body; questioning and trusting yourself, as well as feeling things fully. This chapter is designed to allow you to take each of these notions further and enact both real change *and* action.

Core Principles

As you will now be aware, one of the key goals when working towards sustainable health improvement is to create a baseline, where you can make the right decisions about what is good and bad for you. What needs to be eliminated is everything that ails you, as well as the cloudy external information that gets in the way of you knowing your body and your mind. When you remove all of this, and get to your baseline, you will be able to make correct decisions all the time!

Meditate on the following truths. As you ponder each, you may also come up with your own. At the end of the day, the meaning you give to each of these is even more powerful than if I were to simply define them for you.

You are imperfectly perfect in every respect (soul/spirit, mind and body) Progress is perfection, so make progress no matter how small. Progress has no direction; sometimes it is necessary to go *back*, in order to move *forwards*

A contemplation of each of these notions will help you tap into your innate intuitive intelligence, and make the right decisions. You will develop a sense of presence, allowing you to get in touch with yourself and find this very intelligence within you. This will take time to master, and you will make mistakes on occasion, but that is okay! This is exactly what I want you to reflect on.

Furthermore, remember to refer back to the various exercises so far in this book. The gamma brainwave state exercise, for example, is a great way to be present and get in touch with your subconscious. As well as this, I urge you to frequently revisit the action items provided in each chapter, in addition to the very material within each, as you see fit. Because indeed, no amount of contemplation upon such a crucial topic as health can ever be too much.

With all of that said, let's get into the action plan.

Chapter 11

The 6 Week Challenge

This section of the book is for you to improve 6 areas of your life — 1 per week.

Your job is to simply take action in accordance, one week after the next. At the end of the book, you can find a simple tracking sheet, which will allow you to check off whether you have done what is needed for the corresponding week. This will require daily engagement, enabling you to build consistency.

This challenge is stackable, whereby each week will build that which comes before. It is also sustainable, meaning you can easily continue this for the rest of your life.

There is only 1 rule for this challenge: if you miss a day, you start from the beginning.

The 6 weeks are as follows:

1. Air
2. Water
3. Food
4. Spirit
5. Mind
6. Body

Fundamentally, this challenge is designed to help you take action, and not get stuck in your head. And soon, if you take part with the consistency and effort I know you can, you will find that the real science is how your health will be transformed at the end of the 6 weeks.

All that is left is to just get started...

Week 1

Air

Breathe 5 seconds in, 5 seconds out, and 5 minutes a day. Pay attention to where you are breathing. It should be in your abdomen, not your chest, and it should be deep, proper breathing.

Week 2

Water

Clear to clear: drink pure, filtered water, aiming for clear urine towards the end of the day.

Week 3

Food

Only eat foods you know are good for you. Utilise the hourglass method discussed in Chapter 3 to help guide you as to what these are.

Effectively, good food is natural, not made in a lab.

Do NOT use supplements — you need to get real nutrition from natural food.

Week 4

Mind

Find 5 new positive things in any area of your life. Reflect and meditate on them daily.

Week 5

Spirit

Spend 3 minutes, daily, contemplating experiences in your life to be grateful for.

Week 6

Body

Exercise for 12 minutes each day.

This will vary from person to person, but just find something that is achievable for you.

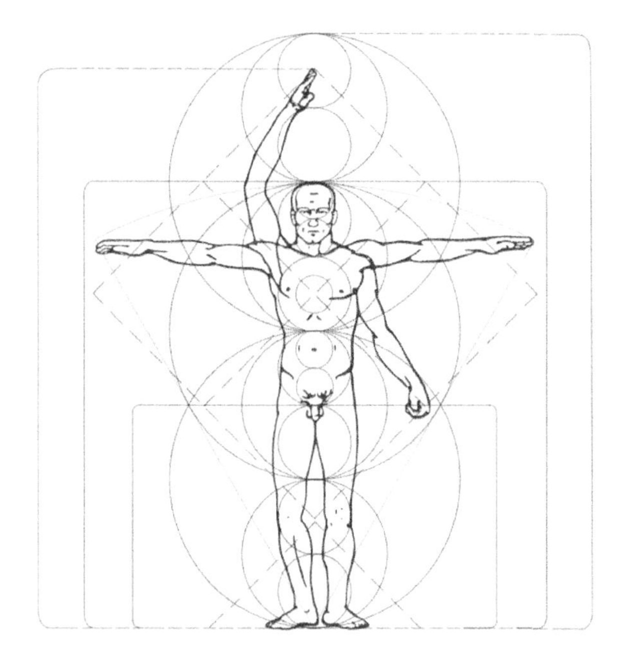

Chapter 12

Tracking Good Health

After this 6-week challenge, you will be well on your way to maintaining a stable health plan that works for you. You will need to see how things react, and adapt accordingly. Take week 6, for example. Gradually extend your exercise time, see how you react, and change accordingly. I do not want to, nor can I, give you too specific of a plan, because you need to work out what is best for you!

What this requires is proper tracking, which will allow you to make the correct decisions.

I have tried to stress some key points several times in this book. These include the notions that you need to; breathe properly; hydrate; eat natural food; listen to your body; understand your subconscious; take control of what is hidden and focus on internal validation. Everything has been linked and focusing on tracking some of these key areas can help you get closer to achieving your health vision, by incorporating them into your routine, and making health a habit.

There are a variety of things you can and should track, and below you can find a useful tracking sheet. One thing to note is that a good physician can help you do more regular, clinical tests, such as checking the functioning of your liver, kidney, other organs as well as blood tests and so on. This will give you an insight into how your body's health is doing, and hopefully, improving!

The things that you can check for yourself, however, include your breathing, hydration, food and mood. First of all, check how often you are doing proper breathing, as you will have come to learn more about throughout. Then, track how much water you drink each day. On top of that, track all the food you are eating. If you do all of this, and you notice a change in your body, you will thus be able to trace it to a change in your breathing, drinking or eating. You will be able to see how all of these different aspects affect you, in order to workout what you need to do to achieve optimal health.

Also, track your mood. Check your emotions, where you are along the scale, what other feelings you have each day, and how you dealt with them. You may identify patterns and see if you are perhaps working towards staying in the adaptive cycle, rather than the maladaptive, and therefore getting healthier with regards to your emotions.

The concept of modifying your thought patterns, behaviours and emotions has been discussed thoroughly throughout.

If you work to try and get in touch with your subconscious, and get rid of these limiting beliefs, you need to see what changes happen there. Perhaps after trying to get in touch with yourself, you will feel in a better mood.

Or maybe you will feel more motivated and have a stronger will to change your behaviours.

Tracking can show you the success of these inspections. Remember, the action items may be helpful in this process. Checking your physical activity is incredibly easy these days through the use of devices and apps. Ensure that you are doing the amount you set for yourself. You should start small and build up, and eventually it will become second nature to you. At the same time, tracking can also give you an idea of what you are doing right and wrong, which can correspond to the results that you may feel.

Why is tracking so important? Because you have data. Memory is incredibly unreliable. We tend to generalise things, string information together and lose the ability to accurately remember what we have done. Because these health habits are small and not always the most exciting, they do not always stand out. We don't remember the daily workout that was neither exciting nor difficult. So, keeping a log every day of all the things you do will give you the data that you can later refer to.

This can also act as a motivational tool. You will be able to see how much work you do every day, while working towards your goal. Sometimes you may think, "Oh I didn't do this, that or the other. I didn't run every day, and therefore I am not doing anything." This thought might make you want to give up.

How to Track More Effectively

Tracking all these things at once may be a bit overwhelming. So, start by first measuring the things most important to you, and you can then add more later as you go along. Also, consider what other people measure, and compare this to your own priorities. Experiment, and see how doing this makes you feel, and perhaps more importantly if it goes towards what you want to achieve. Measuring your weight right away may not be the most important thing to you right now, for example.

Also, try to measure certain things in relation to others. If you are measuring weight, see how it relates to your energy levels. Or what about the exercise you did today, in relation to your mood? Try to draw out the relations between different activities as much as possible. When you see the patterns, you can grow your awareness of the formerly invisible signals you used to ignore. This will ultimately enable you to change things, and take better control of yourself.

How to Know When You are Making Progress

This awareness of progress will ultimately come down to when you fill your life with things that are supportive of health.

When you do, you can the ask yourself key questions, such as:

- *How are you using your time? Is it for this reason?*
- *Do you have more energy?*
- *Do you feel, when you truly inspect yourself, healthier?*
- *Have these actions: eating, drinking, breathing and exercising, become a habit?*

This last point is a major one concerning your progress. Initially, you will start in the area of unconscious incompetence. This means that you don't know; what food is good for you; how much water to drink; what mood you feel; what emotions you are suppressing, and what signals your body is sending you. Then, as you get into developing some expertise in these areas, you will become *consciously* incompetent, though we still have to think about certain things.

There will still be a gap, and this is where having someone that you believe in, like and trust, who can help you, is important. They can fill that gap initially, by directing your attention and helping you find the appropriate resources that will be supportive for you. This essentially means trying to find someone else that can help you identify the things you don't realise, in order to eventually stop being incompetent. Of course, you know yourself best, and this entire process is all about looking inward, but someone else can be useful to help you as you start. Ideally, it should be someone who has good health, that you look up to in this regard, and can see things that you have missed about yourself.

This will allow you to become consciously competent, as you go through and make changes in your daily life. This is where you should have a specific health routine that you are focused on, and can track and measure, which will enable you to make changes that will support your health. At this stage, everything you do will require a conscious effort and some recognition of each act you do, and the things that may still not feel entirely natural. Now, this can be hard, requiring you to put a lot of extra energy into your health. But the more you do it, the closer you will get to it being second nature.

Eventually, when you solidify those habits, you will become unconsciously *competent*. When this is achieved, you can rise to the next level, whereby you don't have to consciously put effort into breathing, drinking and eating well. Instead, you will just do these things without even thinking about them.

You will be aware of your emotions and signals, while in tune and synchronised.

To conclude, I want to talk a little about mastery. Some confuse mastery with recognition. Yet just because you saw something doesn't mean you can do it well. Just because you heard a fact doesn't mean you could automatically understand it on a deeper level. Recognition is the start of mastery.

But to really gain mastery, there are two additional ingredients that are required. Tony Robbins always says that repetition is the mother of skill. During one of his talks I attended, it came to me that if repetition is the mother, then who is the father? In my mind, the father is awareness.

The development of awareness then becomes the father of mastery, because as you become aware you can then begin to tell the slight differences. And as you hone your senses, you will become keenly aware of the things that are happening inside the body. A very simple example is that you cannot control the amount of food you eat if you do not know or are not aware which of those signals is actually hunger or thirst.

A lot of people think that they are hungry because it is a particular time, when instead they might be thirsty or dehydrated. If you've never experienced fasting before, then perhaps hunger is a signal that has been mixed up emotionally, due to the fact that many people misidentify eating and the feeling of fullness with the feeling of either connection or some kind of certainty.

It is important to be specific with what we do and when to achieve mastery. To explain why, I want to talk about Parkinson's Law for a moment. Parkinson's Law suggests that your past expands to fill the time allotted. This is a good way to actually waste time by having an open-ended journey. Therefore, if you said that you were going to exercise this afternoon, and there was no particular defined time, then the afternoon can stretch into the evening and, before you know it, it's already gone, by which point you haven't done anything.

So, what we need to do is put in specific timeframes that can help focus the mind to say, "Okay, this is non-negotiable. This is the time when I am going to take action." When you are learning mastery via repetition, a good, strict routine is a key step to solidifying these events and making them sustainable. No vague instructions to yourself! But, eventually, they will become second nature.

The philosophy that I have is: you are here to make progress. The body is designed to make progress. You go from one cell, to two, four, and all the way to 100 trillion. That is a progression. We then have specialisation of those cells, as indeed they turn to form specific types of tissue, the tissues then turn into organs, and the organs together form a system, which then becomes you as a human being. There is always progress that is being made.

TRACKING SHEET

WEEK 4	AIR	WATER	FOOD	SPIRIT	MIND	BODY
DAY 1						
DAY 2						
DAY 3						
DAY 4						
DAY 5						
DAY 6						
DAY 7						

WEEK 5	AIR	WATER	FOOD	SPIRIT	MIND	BODY
DAY 1						
DAY 2						
DAY 3						
DAY 4						
DAY 5						
DAY 6						
DAY 7						

WEEK 6	AIR	WATER	FOOD	SPIRIT	MIND	BODY
DAY 1						
DAY 2						
DAY 3						
DAY 4						
DAY 5						
DAY 6						
DAY 7						

WEEK 1	AIR	WATER	FOOD	SPIRIT	MIND	BODY
DAY 1						
DAY 2						
DAY 3						
DAY 4						
DAY 5						
DAY 6						
DAY 7						

WEEK 2	AIR	WATER	FOOD	SPIRIT	MIND	BODY
DAY 1						
DAY 2						
DAY 3						
DAY 4						
DAY 5						
DAY 6						
DAY 7						

WEEK 3	AIR	WATER	FOOD	SPIRIT	MIND	BODY
DAY 1						
DAY 2						
DAY 3						
DAY 4						
DAY 5						
DAY 6						
DAY 7						

Conclusion

Welcome to Your Imperfect Perfection

I want us for a moment to think back to the start of the book, where the idea that we are all imperfectly perfect was discussed. This sentiment applies to the ways in which we are both born into and how we navigate through life. Similarly, one's health journey is the same. It is not linear, but will instead be dotted with all kinds of wonderful challenges and synchronicities. But eventually, with the right knowledge and application, we are going to get there.

Health is not a static location; it is a journey. This is a crucial motivation, because whenever you make a mistake, if things go wrong, it isn't the end. We have to keep trying. Throughout this book, I have given you a way to work out your own optimal health plan, and a lot of tips to access your innate intuitive intelligence. However, it is important to remember that this will not be immediate. You will make mistakes, and sometimes you will have to go backward in order to go forward.

However, so long as you work on taking small steps to improve your health, you will eventually be able to achieve your health vision. Take things one step at a time, make them manageable, and listen to your body.

Two different people trying this will end up with very different health plans, diets, exercise plans and routines, because everyone is different. You should not compare yourself to others, nor think that there is some secret ideal plan out there, because there isn't. The only health journey for you to embark on is the one that you create yourself!

One of my final pieces of advice is that you have to distinguish what is fantasy from reality.

Fantasy

The fantasy many people imagine is that the pursuit of health is a matter of going in a straight line from A to B. Yet this can never be the case. You cannot go from being in bad shape and eating badly, to immediately running every day, having a perfect diet and being the embodiment of good health.

A healthy lifestyle has to be sustainable, and it has to be based on your baseline. The same is true for this approach. You will not be perfect immediately, and you cannot expect perfection by doing all of this every day to start with. Instead, you have to take it step by step. Of course, you will sometimes make mistakes, but from these you simply have to continue on.

Reality

A more realistic outcome is having 7 days being perfect, then perhaps you miss a day and start again. When this occurs, you should carry out 1.5 perfect weeks, start again, and then do 2 perfect weeks. Maybe you then give up for 1 week.

If so, that is okay! Recommit, do 3.5 weeks perfectly, and start again. So long as you aim to recommit and try to establish routines and rituals in your life that aim at improving your health, you *will* improve your health.

What this all depends upon is the fundamental realisation that health is *not* a destination, but instead a *journey*, of constant, never-ending improvement. If you continue to develop and make improvements, despite any setbacks, you *will* improve your health.

You need to understand your subconscious, your feelings and your body signals, and view health holistically. From the cells that make us, all the way to your spiritual direction. By doing things in the correct order, in the steps I have laid out, you can learn from yourself, and thus improve both our health and your life drastically.

I hope that you have at the very least come to the end of this book with an understanding that you have the capacity for good health, that you *can* be correct all the time and that you don't need any more advice, fad diets or supplements. That instead, getting to know yourself and sustainable action are all that is needed for good health.

By listening to and understanding yourself, as well as taking the appropriate actions based on what you already know and what your body is telling you, you will achieve better health. This, most important of all, will then enable you to be a better entrepreneur. You will succeed, by synchronising your goals and direction with your body's capacities and mental well-being.

The solution was never anywhere else. Think about it, you're incredible!

The answers are already inside you.

Testimonial

My name is Phil, and I live in Liverpool, UK. I'm a managing director for a large healthcare recruitment business, have three kids, and what can oftentimes be a stressful life! It is my honour, now, to both describe and recommend the services of the brilliant Dr. HB.

HB and I, originally, met through my partner. Now, I've always been a very mainstream individual, while she has often looked at the more alternative things in life. Well, around a year ago, she was beginning to get involved in something she described to me as 'Quantum Energy Coaching'. I had never heard of QEC before, and even remember when she first came to me talking about it, thinking, "Oh my God, what is this?" Soon after, herself beginning the course at the time, she told me that they were looking for volunteers.

My immediate response?

"Absolutely not. Not for me. Not going to do it."

But eventually, I (fortunately!) got a little side-armed into doing it. They were extremely short for volunteers, so I decided, "Okay, I'll give it a go."

Now, in the first couple of sessions, I was really quite closed off to the whole thing. But as I started to do a little more research, and began to talk more to HB himself, I slowly opened up. And then more, and more, began to find that the processes helped me in ways I couldn't imagine.

So, what was I like *before* working with HB? Well, I was daydreaming my way through life, and struggling with my relationship. You know, just going through the motions. Not dealing with my emotions, or feelings, but instead just plodding on through each day, without too much of a thought of what I was *actually* doing. It was just like muscle memory, doing the same things, *day in, day out.*

Difficulties in mine and my partner's relationship had really started to rear their head around the time we started to have children — nearly eight years ago now, with my eldest daughter turning eight next month! Becoming a parent throws a whole host of issues into the frame, and I now realise I simply wasn't equipped to deal with, and tackle, them, with empathy.

It can be a tricky thing to understand the changes your partner's going through, while also facing your own self-doubt. I suppose I even experienced the typical male sensation of, "Well, it's tough to deal with, so let's shut down instead." I buried my head in the sand for so long, hoping that everything would sort itself out. But when you do this, of course it won't.

So, these feelings stayed present, in some shape or form, for eight years. Eight years of having my head buried in the sand, all the while not knowing how to talk about these feelings;

how to approach them. I had a lot of resistance in my own head as to how to deal with these things, always shifting the blame: it's not my fault, it's my partner's. Admittedly, the both of us, on certain occasions, were on the brink of thinking whether or not the relationship would work, and whether we'd be together if it continued on the way it was.

I was completely lost — not just with my partner, but life in general. Constantly asking: where is everything heading? On many occasions, I was close to really thinking about ending our relationship, because I simply did not know how to tackle the issues that we faced, or how to have those honest conversations.

I think that's the fundamental problem for a lot of relationships. You're never going to have one that's *perfect*, but can you deal with the issues? Can you move forward from them, and not just let them fester away as they go on to build up into something even worse? That was the point I had reached, one from which I thought I would not return. I'd allowed certain things, for seven, eight years, to fester and build, without dealing with those issues and problems.

Enter Dr. HB.

QEC work, and his coaching, has allowed me to, first, be able to engage in healthy conversations, before then identifying and taking the issues, in order to deal with them. Now, me and my partner are in a place where we can engage in these healthy conversations, and work through our issues, instead of letting them fester.

Indeed, perhaps the biggest benefit of working with HB is that I am now able to communicate far better with my partner. In the past, I have used all of life's stressors as deflectors, neglecting to deal with the issues in our relationship. And now, the fact that I am dealing with the issues that I had has meant that communication between my partner and I, within our relationship, has dramatically improved.

Now, she initially struggled to believe that I would maintain the changes that I was making! Well, at least regarding our communication. But, you know, I don't blame her! All of this had been going on for such a longtime, and I think it's only human to doubt sustainable change.

But now, we've been able to get our relationship back on track. She's very much pleased with where I am at, and where I'm communicating with her. In fact, she would say that this experience has made just as huge a difference in her life, as well.

QEC work, and his coaching, has allowed me to, first, be able to engage in healthy conversations, before then identifying and taking the issues, in order to deal with them. Now, me and my partner are in a place where we can engage in these healthy conversations, and work through our issues, instead of letting them fester.

Indeed, perhaps the biggest benefit of working with HB is that I am now able to communicate far better with my partner. In the past, I have used all of life's stressors as deflectors, neglecting to deal with the issues in our relationship. And now, the fact that I am dealing with the issues that I had has meant that communication between my partner and I, within our relationship, has dramatically improved.

Now, she initially struggled to believe that I would maintain the changes that I was making! Well, at least regarding our communication. But, you know, I don't blame her! All of this had been going on for such a longtime, and I think it's only human to doubt sustainable change.

But now, we've been able to get our relationship back on track. She's very much pleased with where I am at, and where I'm communicating with her. In fact, she would say that this experience has made just as huge a difference in her life, as well.

My partner's an empath, a talker. She wants to talk deeply, about deeply emotional issues. And, you know, she's paired with this person who was only offering: yes, no — very one-word answers, from someone who was always asking, in turn: why do we even need to deal with these things? Of course, it always takes two to tango. But she can see that I am making that effort to listen, to engage, to take time to talk about things.

This has allowed both of us to have an understanding that, you know, there's always going to be both good times, and bad. Those times when we're able to communicate, better than others. She might want a deep conversation at G in the morning, when we just got up over coffee —unfortunately, that's not the best time to communicate with me! But this all comes down to the healthy boundaries we have been able to establish, for one another, that HB has enabled me to see.

Because absolutely, working with HB has allowed me to have more of this very awareness. To discover the ability to hear my own thoughts, regardless of whatever situation I might find myself in. Whether I'm under stress, with my partner, or in a work situation — I am now consciously aware of what my mind is saying to me, and doing, as it steers me based upon my past experiences and learned behaviours.

Through QEC, I have learned that I do a lot of what my parents did — their bad behaviours, their bad ways of dealing with things. In turn, this has allowed me to become aware of my own reactions, understand that they can be altered, and change them at a subconscious level.

Both at the start, and every step that I've been through on this journey, there were admittedly a lot of down days. But I have found that once you are able to solve communication issues, you are then able to lift the general view, and mood, of how you interact.

It's like anything — nothing can ever be perfect. I still have days where, for whatever reason, I will feel emotionally unregulated. But once you are able to get into a certain space, and think it through, I have found that I can regulate my emotions a hell of a lot better.

HB has enabled me to learn just how to be able to go and figure out what the issue is. To question: why am I thinking a certain way, and what is it that's going on for me right now that's causing these feelings? — In order to then be able to address them.

My emotions are so much more regulated, having learned how to have less of the 'beating yourself up', and those 'down days'. How to trust yourself to get through that period of time, and believe that *you can*. Because We are all human at the end of the day. We are going to have fluctuations, for we are emotional beings. It is what it is.

Of course, just as with anything in life, there is still lots of work to do. But ultimately, the biggest effect from my experience with HB's Quantum Energy Coaching is that I am now far more conscious in my life, and finally dealing with the problems that I've got. Still lots to deal with, on what is an ongoing journey. But beforehand, the problems were there, yet I wasn't even acknowledging, or doing, anything about them. And I now feel like there is *a way to move forward*, with anything I face.

And so, if someone was to say that they were considering whether or not to work with HB, I would answer: you shouldn't even have to think about it!

He has gone over and above to give me support. By being so easy to talk to, all the while offering very practical guidance and advice throughout the process. It's been a pleasure, and I wouldn't hesitate to put forward his services to even those closest to me. Thank you, HB, for everything.

Next Steps

Congratulations entrepreneurs for deciding that you are ready to live in outstanding health!

Click here to begin your FREE Burnout Prevention Masterclass, for the exponential growth of your health. https://www.drhblo.com/webinar

Entrepreneurs, as a gift from me to you, also get your 'Why am I tired all the time' special report. www.Drhblo.com

About The Author

Dr. Hoe Bing Lo, or **HB** as he is affectionately called by all, lives in Cairns, Australia, with his wife Tanya and two children Jason and Jessica.

His family is the reason he does what he does. HB helps people discover their own truths and brilliance, so they can shine even brighter.

During the day, HB works in a private corporate medical clinic as a general physician, specialising in treating and preventing skin cancer. HB created a program, Exponential Health, where you can tap into and use your intuitive healing, through self- re-discovery.